ENDORSEMENTS

When I was a young man, my life was transformed by the Holy Spirit during the charismatic movement. I have nothing but gratefulness in my heart for that season of renewal in the 1970s. But I believe the most mature Christians know that what we saw in the 1970s and 1980s was not the ultimate in revival. We are still waiting for a pure move of the Spirit, one that is not tainted by man's agenda, huge egos, sexual scandals, and the merchandising of God's anointing.

The apostle Paul told the Thessalonians, "But examine everything carefully; hold fast to that which is good; abstain from every form of evil" (1 Thess. 5:22-22). British preacher Charles Spurgeon once said, "You who do not like self-examination are the persons who need it most.... If you search yourselves, and allow the Word of God to search you, it is well with you." In this book, R. T. Kendall does a masterful job of helping us properly assess the past. Those of us who call ourselves charismatics must seriously examine the fruit of our movement, cling to the good, throw out the bad, and pray intently for the promise of genuine spiritual revival. This excellent book will help us do that.

—**J. Lee Grady**
Author, Speaker, and Director of The Mordecai Project

My friend R. T. Kendall is a great gift to the Church. He's given his life to a ministry fully devoted both to Word and Spirit. If his prophetic expectation in this book occurs, we will see the very revival that is the only hope to dethrone the avalanche of spiritual apostasy and cultural idolatry.

—**Mark Driscoll**
Founding Pastor of Trinity Church and RealFaith Ministry

Of the many wonderful books written by Dr. Kendall, this one will perhaps ultimately be known as his magnum opus! When reading the book, I found myself constantly looking up into Heaven with conviction but also with great confidence and courage, while praying, "Oh, Lord Jesus, please let it be so!" As someone converted during the charismatic movement but also having ministered and worked among traditional Pentecostals for the last two decades, I welcome and genuinely celebrate the perspective provided, and look forward to the true Spirit-empowered revival proposed and surely just ahead!

—**Sam Hemby, PhD**
Professor of Practical Theology, Southeastern University

Receiving the

ISAAC PROMISE

R.T. KENDALL

Receiving the

ISAAC
PROMISE

Position Yourself for the Fullness of
God's End-Time Outpouring

DESTINY IMAGE® PUBLISHERS, INC.
P.O. Box 310, Shippensburg, PA 17257-0310
"Publishing cutting-edge prophetic resources to supernaturally empower the body of Christ"

This book and all other Destiny Image and Destiny Image Fiction books are available at Christian bookstores and distributors worldwide.

For more information on foreign distributors, call 717-532-3040.

Reach us on the Internet: www.destinyimage.com.

ISBN 13 TP: 978-0-7684-7398-8

ISBN 13 eBook: 978-0-7684-7399-5

ISBN 13 HC: 978-0-7684-7401-5

ISBN 13 LP: 978-0-7684-7400-8

For Worldwide Distribution, Printed in the U.S.A.

1 2 3 4 5 6 7 8 / 27 26 25 24 23

To Diane Jackson

I dedicate this book to Diane Jackson, the
widow of the late John Paul Jackson.

CONTENTS

FOREWORD

I must admit, after agreeing with R. T. that I would be happy to write a foreword for his new book, *Receiving the Isaac Promise,* I was somewhat taken aback when I realized his opening theme was comparing the charismatic revival to Ishmael. That suggested to me that the whole thing should have never happened. I was fine with the coming of Isaac as a metaphor for a final, massive, and wonderful revival of the Holy Spirit—a perfect fulfillment of the promise of God for an end-time revival and harvest. But I was not willing in the least to compare the charismatic move of God to be an Ishmael. I had to read the entire book before I realized that R. T.'s metaphor of using Ishmael was his way of saying that the charismatic revivals of the last fifty years are incomplete and have had their problems, difficulties, moral failures, etc., of which I readily would agree. My challenge was my belief that Ishmael was actually a carnal mistake on the part of Abraham and Sarah, which led to Ishmael being born of Hagar.

All of this is true, however. Abraham so accepted his son Ishmael that he was happy to love Ishmael as his son and have Ishmael as his heir. A further word to Abraham from the Lord let Abraham know that his actual heir would be born of Sarah. The first son was somewhat flawed, both in the way he was born and then in his nature, character, and behavior, whereas Isaac was born legitimately and behaved in total obedience, as demonstrated during the time he was offered on an altar of sacrifice by his father in Genesis 22:9. Isaac was probably about twelve or thirteen years old at the time and perfectly capable of running away, yet he submitted himself to Abraham's will. Isaac was always recognized by the Lord as the promised heir.

God has promised to the Church, and indeed the whole world, an end-time harvest. Jesus said the harvest is at the end of the age, and the angels are the reapers, implying that the end-time harvest will be the greatest ingathering of all time (see Matt. 13:39). I needed to read this entire volume before I finally understood and agreed with R. T.'s analogy.

God has definitely saved the best wine until now. The end-time harvest will indeed surpass what happened in the days of the early church. What we have had thus far *has* been imperfect and incomplete. Any time now, we are about to enter unparalleled times of supernatural healings, conversions, and harvest on a global scale, which will be unprecedented to anything we have seen heretofore. As we look around our world today and see the extraordinary global advancement of the Kingdom of God on the one hand, and the multiplicity of insurmountable political and geological problems on the other, then surely we can agree—the end of the age is upon us.

Additionally, Dr. Kendall takes the opportunity to point out the faults and weaknesses of our present-day charismatic revival and moving of the Holy Spirit. There is far too much false doctrine, compromise, and lukewarmness, not to mention the serious lack of biblical knowledge and sound doctrine. This has seriously impinged the impact and influence of our present-day revivals and clearly must be rectified in order to restore the integrity and impact that God requires and desires.

The integrity of the Word of God and of the holiness and standards of God Himself must be restored in the minds of Christian people in particular and to the world itself in general. The message of the Christian gospel with all its hope and promise must be holding forth integrity and godly character exemplified in the lives of its messengers. I think it is fitting that Dr. Kendall be one of these gospel champions as he has stood for integrity and godly character throughout his entire life and ministry, along with an uncompromising and clear presentation of the good news of Jesus Christ.

This book is a very needed and important volume, and I encourage you to read it carefully through to the end. It does not overly focus on the shortcomings of the charismatic movement but on the coming promised harvest (see Rev. 14:14-15). We do need, however, to take the necessary correction into our hearts and lives so that we can truly be ready for this mighty move that God is preparing for His Bride, the Church. God is about to make us *the head and not the tail* (Deut. 28:13). The Lord will lead us into the most exciting and fruitful season of revival that any of us have ever read about or considered, while at the same time getting all of us ready for His glorious return.

Get ready, friends; the Church's finest hour is just ahead!

—**John G. Arnott**
Founder, Catch the Fire World, Toronto

FOREWORD

Over the last thirty years or more, R. T. Kendall and I have often sat down together to discuss theological ideas, including those which led to the publication of *Receiving the Isaac Promise*. On October 16, 1992, I was in London's Wembley Conference Centre when R. T. first publicly presented his metaphorical connection between Ishmael and the charismatic movement.

It was a controversial event. In Galatians 4, the apostle Paul associated Ishmael with religious legalism, a fleshly bondage which must be cast out. Now R. T. was saying Charismatics *were* Ishmael! Some never got past their initial shock. After all, R. T. is a renowned expository preacher and always endeavors to draw out the true meaning and intent of the text before him. But here he was clearly making connections that the apostle Paul never expressly made.

Many leaders had enthusiastically embraced the charismatic movement, delighting in a fresh experience of the Holy Spirit and the fruitfulness that followed. Extending beyond the boundaries of classical Pentecostal churches, the renewal had penetrated practically every historic denomination. It seemed to many that this move was the final revival of church history. However, growing numbers of Charismatics today are ready to accept that what we have experienced up to now is not all that God is going to do.

R. T. believes that the charismatic movement is certainly not the final move of God on planet Earth. Something far greater is coming which will eclipse it both in intensity and ultimate purpose. The great awakening to come will bring in the final harvest and prepare the Bride of Christ for the coming of the Bridegroom. The Church of the last days is going to be holy, powerful, faithful, glorious, and vigorously opposed by the world. The difference between this and the former charismatic movement will be as stark as the difference between Isaac and Ishmael.

Though Ishmael was blessed, he was not the promised offspring. We are not to look back or sentimentally hold on to Ishmael. We are to rejoice and be ready for Isaac. Isaac, R. T. argues, is a prophetic picture of the final, greatest move of God that will happen immediately before the second coming of Christ. It will be chiefly associated with the restoration of powerful preaching of the pure gospel. The final harvest will be great both in geographical scope and spiritual impact. Jesus will be honored, and God will be glorified across the earth. There will be an upsurge of incontrovertible signs, wonders, and miracles— greater than at any time since the days of the early church.

Some may be skeptical about a final awakening in the last days. There are, broadly speaking, two views that dominate eschatological thinking among evangelicals. The one tends toward defeatism and the other toward triumphalism. We must take into account both the Scriptures which point to apostasy and coldness at the end of the age, and those which speak of a more positive scenario.

I am in agreement with R. T. God's people will rise up, the authentic gospel will be preached with genuine spiritual impact, and the final harvest will be gathered. God will be glorified in the Church. The gospel will prevail. There will be a great awakening as presented in the midnight cry of the parable of the ten virgins. This is not triumphalism. R. T. recognizes that there will be those who reject Christ and will also oppose the gospel and vigorously persecute those who preach it. The coming revival will be a definitive manifestation of the Kingdom of Christ on earth. Christ must reign in Heaven until His enemies have become His footstool. The revival will prepare the world for the full consummation of His Kingdom.

Of particular interest is R. T.'s understanding of the role that Romans 4 will have in this revival. The preaching of justification by faith alone set the early church on fire and, in the sixteenth century, brought about a historic Reformation impacting much of the world and setting the stage for further historic moves of God like the Great Awakening on both sides of the Atlantic. This same message, as presented in the first part of Romans 4, will once again be center stage in Christian life and ministry. The message of the second part of Romans 4 will also ignite revival fires. This will put the holiness of God's people high on the agenda. It will focus on the obedience necessary for us to enter into our inheritance, just as it was for Abraham. Sanctification will be taken as seriously as justification in the move of God to come, as it has in every historic revival. But, this time, it will be more complete and more evident than at any other time since the apostles of the first century.

This, then, is the thesis of R. T.'s book. I commend it to you and pray that it will not only be a message well-received, but also be used of the Lord as a catalyst for the events of which it speaks.

—**Colin Dye**
Senior Minister,
Kensington Temple London City Church, London

PREFACE

his is my first book with Destiny Image. I am amazed at their courage. Their clientele is largely Charismatic. In this book, I call the charismatic movement *Ishmael,* the future move of the Spirit I call *Isaac.* My publisher, Larry Sparks, affirms the charismatic movement, as I do.

However, we believe there is more. That is what this book is about. I need to say urgently, the reader needs to be familiar with the parable of the ten virgins in Matthew 25:1-13. I plead with you to read these thirteen verses over and over again if you are not familiar with them. My case is based largely on this parable.

I want to thank John Arnott for graciously agreeing to write the encouraging foreword. I have known John and Carol for twenty years, having spoken a number of times at the Toronto Airport Fellowship.

Colin Dye has kindly written a foreword for British readers. Colin was the senior pastor of Kensington Temple for over thirty years. He was actually present at the first Word and Spirit conference in October 1992.

I am deeply indebted to Alyn Jones, a protégé of John and Carol, for his immensely helpful comments in my writing this book. Some readers may recall that I dedicated my book *Prophetic Integrity* (Thomas Nelson) to Alyn and A. J., his wife.

I want to express gratitude to Larry Sparks and the publishing team at Destiny Image. Working with their staff and my editor Edie Mourey has been a joy.

Most of all, my thanks to Louise—my best friend and critic—for her faithful wisdom.

—**R. T. Kendall**
Nashville, Tennessee

INTRODUCTION

T*he charismatic movement is Ishmael, but Isaac is coming.* This was the focus of the message I gave on October 16, 1992, at the Wembley Conference Centre in London. Taking my text from Genesis 17, I thought it would be thrilling—a big hit! I was wrong.

Twenty-five hundred people came from all over London that day to the first Word and Spirit conference. Chaired by Lyndon Bowring, the late Paul Cain (1929–2019) and I were the speakers. Each of us spoke three times. I was billed to represent the Word, Paul the Spirit. Graham Kendrick wrote a hymn for us, "Jesus Restore to Us Again"—a tremendous song.

Only a few appreciated the message, including Rev. Colin Dye, the respected senior pastor of Kensington Temple, the flagship church of the Elim Pentecostal Church. The auditorium was filled largely with Charismatics and Pentecostals. "You call us Ishmael," some of my best friends and most distinguished charismatic leaders reminded me.

"Yes," I agreed. "But Isaac is coming."

But that—then—did not diffuse them. They were indignant by being referred to as Ishmael. I fully understood that; many of them had indeed paid a great price—being persecuted, marginalized, isolated, and rejected by traditional Christians because of their stand for the direct witness of the Holy Spirit and the availability of the spiritual gifts. They were in no mood to be compared with Ishmael, Abraham's firstborn son. They were not ready in those days for any teaching that said the greatest awakening in the history of the Church was mostly *future*. Many Charismatics sincerely believed—some still believe—that the charismatic movement is *the* final work of God in the last days before the second coming. That an awakening apart from them was coming down the road was not appealing to some of them.

I was surprised, therefore, when Destiny Image asked me to write this very book. But I still hesitated. I cautioned them that I had already put in print in at least two or three places my conviction that the charismatic movement is Ishmael. I feared readers would not be interested in hearing of my experiences and views again. But the publisher knew that and encouraged me to share my conviction about the charismatic movement and what I believe is coming—soon: the greatest move of the Holy Spirit in the history of the Christian Church.

There has been another shift in some people's thinking in the last several years—precipitated by two things. First, the awareness that in 1947 Smith Wigglesworth (1859–1947) evidently had prophesied the same thing as I did on October 16, 1992—which I knew nothing about at the time—has caused some people to rethink their prejudices. But there is more. An ever-increasing number of charismatic leaders are now saying in so many words, "If what we have now is all there is, we are in pretty bad shape." Indeed, one of the major British charismatic leaders, Gerald Coates (1944–2022), founder of Pioneer, a network of "new" churches, who had been very upset when he first heard my address on October 16, 1992, has since expressed this to me personally.

You will see that I refer fairly often to my chief mentor, Dr. Martyn Lloyd-Jones (1899–1981). He was the minister of Westminster Chapel for thirty years. He put me there in 1977. I refer to him often in my book *Holy Fire* (Charisma House), which is my refutation of "cessationism," the view that purports the gifts of the Spirit are not available today. He was highly esteemed by Pentecostals and Charismatics in Britain. Probably the greatest preacher since Charles Spurgeon (1834–1892), the "Doctor," as he was called (he was a medical doctor before entering the ministry), was like a father to me.

These things said, I urge you to consider prayerfully the burden of this book. This book is not meant to be a criticism of the charismatic movement—of which I am a part—but meant to be an encouragement for those who may have lost hope that God has a definite plan and purpose for the future. Some people call me a Reformed Charismatic. Please do not let any theological disagreement you may have with me put you off. I am *not* motivated to change your theology. I have written this book in my old age (87) to encourage you and give you hope—great hope.

God has a will of His own. He works all things *"according to the counsel of his will"* (Eph. 1:11). Not only does nothing take Him by surprise, but He sees the end from the beginning. He chose Abraham, knowing exactly what Abraham would do. The God of the Bible does not change (see Mal. 3:6). Indeed, *"Jesus Christ is the same yesterday and today and forever"* (Heb. 13:8).

The future is bright. Things may look dark at the moment. Very dark. But the best is yet to come. The very best. How long will it be? Not long.

This book is based on a metaphor, a figure of speech. It is a kind of parable. An allegory. Isaac is a symbol of the greatest revival in the history of the Church. I am not a prophet. I am a Bible teacher. But this book could be a prophetic book. Only time will tell.

For the earth will be filled with the knowledge of the glory of the Lord as the waters cover the sea.
—Habakkuk 2:14

Persons are suspicious of what they have not felt themselves.
—Jonathan Edwards (1703–1758)

Chapter One

IS IT IN THE BIBLE?

M y family and I moved to Oxford, England, on September 1, 1973. We were there for me to do research at Regent's Park College, Oxford, on English Puritanism. A few weeks later, I was surprised to see a notice that the Rev. David du Plessis (1905–1987) from South Africa, known as "Mr. Pentecost," regarded by some as one of the founders of the charismatic movement, would be speaking at a public meeting in the city of Oxford the following Saturday evening—a meeting separate from the university. My old friend and mentor evangelist Rolfe Barnard (1904–1969) used to speak favorably about him. Therefore, I was anxious to hear Mr. du Plessis. It would also be the first time I attended a charismatic meeting.

But I was not impressed. Perhaps I expected too much. For some reason, a sinking feeling came over me. It immediately made me think of an occasion I had attended ten years before. I was pastor of the Fairview Church of God (headquarters in Anderson, Indiana), in Carlisle, Ohio, for eighteen months—from July 1962 to December 1963. I was invited to a ministers' meeting in nearby Middletown, Ohio. Rev. Harald Bredesen (1918–2006), featured in *Time* magazine as a leader of the glossolalia movement (as it was called in those days, based on the Greek word *glossa*—tongue), was in town to share how he was baptized with the Holy Spirit and spoke in tongues. By coincidence, I was seated at the table across from him. He told me that he was a five-point Calvinist, a minister of the Reformed Church in America. That got my attention. He wanted to lay hands on me to receive the baptism of the Holy Spirit. I told him that I had already been baptized by the Holy Spirit.

My baptism in the Holy Spirit came on October 31, 1955, while driving alone in my car from Palmer to Nashville, Tennessee. I entered into what I called the "rest of faith," based on Hebrews 4:10, which I will say more about below. I did not speak in tongues then. But four months later, in February 1956, while driving in my car—this time with four other people—I suddenly felt a welling up in my stomach that wanted to come out. The only way for it to come out was when I began to speak aloud in an unintelligible sound. I instantly realized I had just spoken in tongues. Although it was supernatural, I found it embarrassing that others in the car heard me. They were all Nazarenes and biased against speaking in tongues. But nothing was said.

I kept it to myself for many years. However, I shared this with Rev. Harald Bredesen, that this experience came passively but did not happen again. He said it could indeed happen again and wanted to pray for me that it would return. I always said that, if I ran into a true Calvinist who spoke in tongues, I would listen to him.

I knelt at an altar in the church auditorium where the luncheon was held. I said this to the Lord: "If this is of You, let it come; if not, stop it." I meant those words with all my heart.

Rev. Bredesen then prayed. Nothing happened. He said, "Well?"

I too said, "Well?"

He then made this suggestion: "Take the Scripture literally, 'Make a joyful noise unto the Lord.'"

I said, "I'm not sure what you mean."

He said, "Make a joyful noise. Just make a noise."

This seemed odd.

He said, "Let's pray again."

I listened and would have welcomed whatever the Lord wanted to impart. But nothing happened.

Rev. Bredesen appeared to be a bit frustrated. He said, "Brother Kendall, before the Lord could work with Peter, He had to have a vessel."

I said, "You've got me here on my knees. I am as open as I know how to be."

He now seemed a little bit agitated. He said again, "Make a joyful noise. Just make a noise. Say, 'Ah.'"

I said, "Ah."

"Is nothing happening?" he asked.

"Not yet," I said. I began to feel somewhat scolded by him that nothing happened. I stood up. I said to Rev. Bredesen, "You told me you were a Calvinist. What happened to me on October 31, 1955, and in February 1956, came to me completely passively and unexpectedly without my having to work it up. But you are telling me I must *make it happen*." I gave up and went home.

By sheer coincidence, I ran into him the next day in a restaurant. He said he had been praying for me. He added that his method had always worked before when he prayed for people to receive the gift of tongues.

In my disappointment at the charismatic meeting in Oxford in the fall of 1973—which reminded me of my time with Rev. Bredesen— while listening to David du Plessis, the idea that the charismatic movement was Ishmael was borne in me. I was reminded of Harald Bredesen's effort to work up speaking in tongues. Despite Rolfe Barnard's admiration for David du Plessis, my heart sank. I felt I had missed nothing by not being a part of the charismatic movement. Despite my own real experience of having spoken in tongues in February 1956, I felt no connection with what I witnessed. I did not feel the presence of God that Saturday evening.

In the weeks that followed, the conviction and idea that the charismatic movement was Ishmael—but Isaac was coming—developed. As we shall see below, Ishmael was the result of Abraham's impatient effort to make the promise of a son happen. Ishmael was a non-starter from the beginning as God always had Isaac in mind.

I don't want to be unfair. I am sure that God had used Rev. Harald Bredesen all over the world and that his method worked countless times. Not only that, as I say in my book *Holy Fire*, I myself have come to terms with the fact that God has indeed truly imparted the gift of tongues to people by getting them to initiate a language not their own like Harald Bredesen was suggesting to me.

JACKIE PULLINGER

Jackie Pullinger, aged 79, whom I know quite well, is a living legend of Hong Kong. An upper-middle-class English lady, Jackie felt called to be a missionary while in her early twenties. No society would accept her. She was somehow led to Hong Kong on her own. She became famous for her rehabilitation work with drug addicts. She has not only led thousands of people to the Lord but immediately gets them to receive the gift of tongues.

Jackie told me how she works with drug addicts who live in the slums and streets of Hong Kong. She first presents the gospel to them. If they confess that Jesus died on the cross for their sins and was raised from the dead, she immediately urges them, "Start speaking in a language not your own." They do. They begin speaking in tongues. She then works with them for weeks and months.

I have been to Jackie's place of ministry in Kowloon and have seen what she does with newly converted people who are coming off drugs. Her success rate with drug addicts has been so phenomenal that the city of Hong Kong has given her use of facilities. Indeed, it is greater than that of physicians who use medicine to get addicts off drugs. She has been given the MBE award by Her Majesty Queen Elizabeth II. The explanation for Jackie's success in a word, strange as it may seem, is *getting drug addicts to speak in tongues.*

A Brief History of Pentecostalism and the Charismatic Movement

It is outside the scope of this book to give many historical details of the rise of the Pentecostal movement and the charismatic movement. I would direct the reader to historian Vincent Synan (1934–2020) for those interested in digging deeper into the history of these movements. I met Dr. Synan and spent several hours with him, and afterward corresponded with him. He had mixed feelings about my view that the charismatic movement was Ishmael. Like many at first, he was not happy with my position, but eventually he made it clear to me that he wanted to be included with those who accepted what I teach about Ishmael and Isaac.

Although there is considerable theological reciprocity in the Pentecostal and charismatic movements, they are not the same denominationally or culturally. There has also been a tiny bit of rivalry between the two—but never serious. I have heard some Pentecostals say, "We were there first," referring to the gifts of the Spirit and the weight of being marginalized throughout the twentieth century by traditional Christians like Baptists, Methodists, Presbyterians, Lutherans, and Episcopalians. I also sometimes sensed a measure of resentment by Pentecostals toward Charismatics who are largely made up of the previously mentioned denominations that seemed to be more respected generally than Pentecostals.

The Pentecostal movement sprung out of the Azusa Street revival in Los Angeles in 1906. Denominations like the Assemblies of God, Church of God, Church of God of Prophecy, and the Pentecostal

Holiness Church trace their origins to the Azusa Street revival. That revival—which lasted until 1916—began through the leadership of the African American preacher William J. Seymour (1870–1922). Seymour, if anyone, is often regarded as the founder of the modern Pentecostal movement.

There is no one single founder of the charismatic movement. It would seem that it began in various parts of the world in the early 1960s. Harald Bredesen, like David du Plessis, is widely regarded as an early leader of the charismatic movement, although du Plessis was once a part of the Pentecostal movement in South Africa. The Episcopal minister Dennis Bennett (1917–1991) is often regarded as the founder of the charismatic movement in America. He was moved from an Episcopal church in Los Angeles to Seattle, having been persecuted by his Los Angeles bishop for teaching the baptism of the Spirit and speaking in tongues. He was offered a dying Episcopal church in Seattle that flourished under Bennett's leadership. I never met Rev. Bennett, but Louise and I became close friends of some of his members in Seattle. They spoke often and fondly of Mr. Bennett.

The Rev. Michael Harper (1931–2010), who was on the staff of All Soul's Church, London, is generally regarded as the founder of the charismatic movement in England. He was on the staff at All Soul's, Langham Place, London, when Dr. John Stott (1921–2011) was the rector. Michael Harper received the baptism of the Holy Spirit and spoke in tongues. Dr. Stott, whom I knew well, opposed the teaching of Michael Harper. Harper fell out with Stott and resigned from All Soul's. He founded the Fountain Trust to spread the charismatic message. I was introduced to Michael Harper by my first publisher, Edward England. Michael later joined the Greek Orthodox Church.

David Watson (1933–1984), vicar of St. Michael le Belfrey, York, "one of the best-known clergymen in England," said J. I. Packer (1926–2020), received the baptism of the Spirit and spoke in tongues. His church grew to several hundred. Probably more than anyone in his day, David Watson made the charismatic movement popular in England. He and I were scheduled to have lunch on the very day he received word that he had inoperable cancer. Sadly, I never met him. He had welcomed John Wimber (1934–1997) to England. Afterward, Wimber came to London's Holy Trinity, Brompton (HTB), a number of times. Wimber brought some prophetic men to HTB. This is how I met people like Paul Cain, Bob Jones (1931–2014), and John Paul Jackson (1950–2015).

Later, in April 1994, the "Toronto Blessing" spread to HTB. This was characterized by people uncontrollably falling on the floor and often laughing. It was the London *Sunday Telegraph* that gave the Toronto Blessing its name. The news of this was soon reported in the London *Times*. It spread all over England and eventually to Westminster Chapel. In a sense, HTB and Westminster Chapel became like sister churches. Their vicar in the 1990s, Sandy Millar—who was appointed a bishop after retiring—and his successor Nicky Gumbel—who recently retired—invited me to speak for them several times. HTB is now the largest and fastest growing Anglican church in the United Kingdom. The present Archbishop of Canterbury, Justin Welby, is unashamedly charismatic and a product of HTB.

A HUGE DIFFERENCE IN CHARISMATIC MOVEMENTS

A huge difference between the charismatic movement in England and the charismatic movement in the United States is that in England it is mainstream and widely respected; in America, it is generally regarded as the lunatic fringe of Christianity and largely disdained. I wonder if the reason is partly that the Pentecostal churches in America started with the lower classes, but in England the charismatic movement started with the upper class.

Whereas the Pentecostal movement began with the Azusa Street Revival in Los Angeles in 1906, the charismatic movement, being inter-denominational, is generally assumed to have begun in at least three countries—South Africa, Britain, and America—in around 1960. What was known at first as the glossolalia movement in America at some stage became known as the charismatic movement. The word *charismatic* comes from the Greek word *charismata,* which means "grace gifts."

Why didn't Harald Bredesen's method work with me? I don't know. I can only speculate. But I know in my heart that I was utterly open before God with Rev. Bredesen and very willing to renew speaking in tongues. It just didn't happen with me at that time.

I kept my experience of speaking in tongues to myself for many years. One of the first I told was Dr. Martyn Lloyd-Jones, who put me in Westminster Chapel and was my chief mentor. I was afraid he might reject my experience. On the contrary, he affirmed that what happened to me was of God. It is well known in Britain that both Pentecostals and Charismatics regarded "the Doctor" as a true friend.

I was brought up in the Church of the Nazarene. Many people don't know that the original name of my old denomination was Pentecostal Church of the Nazarene, founded in Pilot Point, Texas, in 1908. This denomination was Wesleyan and regarded the baptism of the Holy Spirit as entire sanctification—meaning heart purity—and not related to tongues. Partly because the Azusa Street revival in Los Angeles was largely associated with speaking in tongues, Nazarenes testified to a different kind of experience and did not want to be associated with Pentecostals. They removed the name Pentecostal in 1919. The consequence of this has been that Nazarenes became anti-Pentecostal. My first pastor in Ashland, Kentucky, told me that he honestly felt that speaking in tongues was of the devil. Many Nazarenes have felt this way. You can imagine, therefore, how I wanted to keep quiet about my own speaking in tongues. But when I felt affirmed by Dr. Lloyd-Jones, I was more willing to share this.

Jackie Pullinger agreed with Harald Bredesen's way. She said that I could indeed speak in tongues. She prayed for me in Hong Kong, but nothing happened. But some years later, while I was still the minister of Westminster Chapel, I recalled Jackie's method with drug addicts. I happened to find myself in a very deep spiritual crisis at one stage. In those days, I used Rob Parson's flat in London to work on sermons. On one afternoon, I felt utterly desperate. I began to plead with the Lord with all my heart to come to my rescue. That is when I remembered what Jackie Pullinger had said. I did what I thought I would never do: I began speaking aloud in Rob's flat in unintelligible sounds. Some would call it gibberish. But something extraordinary followed: *Speaking in tongues flowed*. It was accompanied with a supernatural manifestation that mirrored what happened in February 1956. I have been speaking in tongues ever since—daily, sometimes hourly.

After becoming the pastor of Westminster Chapel, Dr. Lloyd-Jones opened his home to me. I met with him for two hours every Thursday—11 a.m. to 1 p.m.—mostly going over my sermon preparation for the following weekend. I dare say it was the greatest privilege given to any preacher in the history of the Christian Church. We were like father and son. One day, I told him that I regarded the charismatic movement as Ishmael, but that something stupendous was coming. Like Isaac the son that God promised to Abraham. He was intrigued. He did not explicitly say he agreed. But he nodded with implicit affirmation.

Afterward, I stated this publicly several times at Westminster Chapel. One person wrote to me in May 1982 and accused me of turning to Ishmael and not waiting for Isaac to come because I invited Arthur Blessitt to Westminster Chapel! So when I gave my address at Wembley Conference Centre, those Chapel members who were present had already heard it before. But it was new to everyone else.

SIXTY YEARS LATER

I close this first chapter with an observation. The early Pentecostals were born in revival. The emphasis was on the Holy Spirit, speaking in tongues, and healing. That was in 1906. In around 1960 in various parts of the world, there emerged the charismatic renewal. It came in different countries and denominations. As we saw above, this was initially nicknamed the glossolalia movement because the emphasis was on the baptism of the Holy Spirit and especially speaking in tongues. Although the Pentecostals and Charismatics were separate and distinct, they held in common essentially the same emphases: belief in the gifts of the Spirit, especially the gift of tongues.

I need to point out that some Pentecostals do not want to align themselves with Charismatics. That said, I invite you to consider the difference generally in emphasis in 1960 and present time. What follows, I must say, possibly characterizes America more than anywhere else. The main emphasis of Pentecostals and Charismatics in 1960 everywhere was *tongues*. But today, probably more so in the United States, if one goes by the teaching of the more famous television personalities and the better-known charismatic leaders, one seldom hears as much preaching about speaking in tongues or even the gifts of the Spirit generally—unless it is prophecy.

I ask, then, what is the emphasis with so many charismatic leaders today? It seems to me that it is largely *prosperity teaching*. We live in the "Me generation," the "What's in it for me?" generation. No one seems to ask, "What's in it for God?" One is also encouraged to believe that the blessing of God will come in proportion to one's financial support. I'm sorry, but the emphasis is often largely about money. Even the famous TV preachers who were initially known as healing evangelists at some stage for some reason shifted the emphasis to prosperity teaching.

The late Paul Cain, to whom I refer in my book *Prophetic Integrity*, was right in the middle of the healing era of the early 1950s. He shared countless stories of people being healed when he was a boy evangelist.

He said it was common for people with polio to be healed, goiters healed, cancers healed, and hundreds of people came to the tent meetings in wheelchairs and either left them at the tent or carried them home! Paul showed me pictures of people who were healed, photos of wheelchairs that were left. But, said Paul, the healing anointing lifted, and most healing evangelists carried on but didn't want to admit that the healing anointing had largely ended. This, according to Paul, was when he became somewhat of a recluse and was relatively unknown for many years.

These healing evangelists are good people. I have known some of them. Oral Roberts (1918–2009) welcomed me into his home in California three times before he died. He wrote forewords to two of my books. I believe that many of the healing evangelists have been sovereignly raised up of God. In my opinion, many of them have had an undoubted anointing of the Holy Spirit. Some of them have richly blessed Louise and me. I thank God for the way the Pentecostal message and the charismatic renewal have blessed the world generally—especially in Latin America, South America, Africa, China, and Australia.

That said, the message I wish to convey in this book is that the charismatic movement was never raised up to be the ultimate work of God before the end. I believe there is more and better yet to come. Much more. And much better.

I need to make two observations at this stage. You will know what a table is like when the legs of the table are not always exactly the same height. The table wobbles. But the table is still useful. First, as most Bible teachers would say, the parables of Jesus do not stand equally "on all fours," but we need to focus on the main purpose of the parable. We ought to do the same with the thesis of this book. Second, I regard the charismatic movement more than the Pentecostal movement as Ishmael, although there is clearly a lot of overlapping between the two. It would be wrong to push the distinction too far, however.

HABAKKUK 2:14

The prophecy of Habakkuk 2:14—the glory of the Lord shall cover the earth *"as the waters cover the sea"*—is unfulfilled. Either Habakkuk spoke for God—or he didn't. Either the Bible is true—or it isn't. Either God will keep His word—or He won't. My whole life and hope are based upon the premise that God is faithful and true. What I write about in this book will take place. Soon. I hope to be alive—at least in the beginning of it—when it happens.

But when will this be fulfilled? Some think it will come *after* the second coming. I believe it will come *before* the second coming. The greatest move of the Holy Spirit will be orchestrated by Jesus Christ the Son of God while He is *still seated* at the right hand of the Father. He will *stay there* and *remain there* until He makes His enemies His footstool (see Ps. 110:1; Acts 2:34-35; 1 Cor. 15:25; Heb. 1:13). Not every person in the next great move of God will be saved. Not everyone was saved in the first generation of the Church. But the coming of Isaac will cause the world to know that God's Son is on His throne and in control. *Then* Jesus will come in the clouds, and *"every eye shall see him"* (Rev. 1:7 KJV).

It is my belief that the next thing to take place on God's schedule is not the second coming but the awakening of the Church—the coming of Isaac—just prior to the second coming. Then the end will come. I will show this in more detail in the ensuing pages.

I turn now to the historical accounts of Abraham, Ishmael, and Isaac as recorded in the book of Genesis.

After these things the word of the Lord came to Abram in a vision: "Fear not, Abram, I am your shield; your reward shall be very great." But Abram said, "O Lord God, what will you give me, for I continue childless, and the heir of my house is Eliezer of Damascus?" And Abram said, "Behold, you have given me no offspring, and a member of my household will be my heir." And behold the word of the Lord came to him: "This man [Eliezer] *shall not be your heir; your very own son shall be your heir." And he* [God] *brought him* [Abraham] *outside and said, "Look toward heaven, and number the stars, if you are able to number them." Then he* [God] *said to him* [Abraham], *"So shall your offspring be." And he* [Abraham] *believed the Lord, and he* [God] *counted it to him as righteousness.*

—Genesis 15:1-6

God never made a promise that was too good to be true.
—D. L. Moody (1837–1899)

Chapter Two

THE PROMISE TO ABRAHAM

W hen God said to Abraham that his servant Eliezer would not be his heir but that Abraham himself would be a father, it was a promise that seemed too good to be true. However, it was not the first time God promised this to Abraham. But it is the first time that it is written that Abraham "believed" the promise. Abraham was near the age of eighty, Sarah seventy. Sarah was surely too old to bear a child. But Abraham believed God's statement.

This was not a conditional prophecy; there was no "if" implied. This would be true even if Abraham had not embraced it. It was a statement of unconditional truth: Abraham's seed would be countless. It was an unsought word that came from the all-wise and omnipotent God. It is not possible for God to lie (see Titus 1:2; Heb. 6:18). Truth is part of His unchanging nature. It would seem, therefore, that Abraham's seed would have been innumerable as the stars in the Heaven and the sand on the seashore even if Abraham had not believed the statement. But he *did* believe it, and this became the basis for Paul's teaching of justification by faith.

The promise came to Abraham when he was discouraged. He was a wealthy man. It shows that rich people can be discouraged. Many think that having a lot of money means inevitable happiness. No. So why was Abraham discouraged? It was because he had no heir to leave his wealth to. I am sure there would have been a lot of volunteers if Abraham let this word spread. He assumed he would leave his wealth to his servant Eliezer. This assumption gave him no joy. God's word came to Abraham during a vision he was given. The Lord said, *"Fear not, Abram* [as he was called in those days], *I am your shield; your reward shall be very great"* (Gen. 15:1). I choose, however, to call him Abraham from now on since the New Testament does.

What had Abraham done to merit a *"very great"* reward? The answer is, he had been obedient. The Lord at first told him to leave his native country and go to a land the Lord would show him (see Gen. 12:1). Abraham had no idea where that land would be. Indeed, he obeyed *"by faith,"* not even *"knowing where he was going"* (Heb. 11:8)! Such faith pleases God (see Heb. 11:6). When Abraham came to Canaan, God witnessed to him, *"To your offspring I will give this land"* (Gen. 12:7). Abraham must have implicitly believed God then because *"he built an altar to the Lord and called upon the name of the Lord"* (Gen. 12:8). But this is not when God imputed righteousness to him. This does show that Abraham had a prayer life—a relationship with God.

But Abraham was far from perfect. When he and his wife, Sarah, went to Egypt owing to a famine, Abraham made his wife lie to Pharoah because she was beautiful, telling Pharaoh that she was Abraham's sister. Abraham had assumed Pharaoh would kill him. This also suggests that Abraham gave into unbelief and had not sufficiently believed the promise that he would have offspring in Canaan. Otherwise, he would not have made Sarah lie to Pharaoh. And yet Abraham's idea backfired. Pharaoh took Sarah to be his wife! But God afflicted Pharaoh and his house with plagues, and consequently, Pharoah ordered Abraham and Sarah to leave Egypt (see Gen. 12:10-20).

God repeated the promise again. Having returned from Egypt to Canaan, He gave Abraham yet another promise:

> *All the land that you see I will give to you and to your offspring forever. I will make your offspring as the dust of the earth, so that if one can count the dust of the earth, your offspring also can be counted* (Genesis 13:15-16).

There is no explicit indication that Abraham believed this repeated promise. He may have, but possibly in his head, not his heart. The faith that counts is from the *"heart"* (Rom. 10:9-10). In any case, Abraham's folly in Egypt had not changed God's promise or relationship to him.

In Genesis 14, it is recorded that Abraham faced another challenge. He got caught in a crossfire in a war with kings. When they captured his nephew Lot, Abraham got involved. He took 318 of his men and not only rescued Lot but defeated all the kings! It was at this juncture in Abraham's life that the king of Salem, called Melchizedek the priest of "God Most High," brought out bread and wine. To show his gratitude to God for the wonderful victory, Abraham gave one tenth of everything to Melchizedek. This is the origin of the biblical teaching of tithing.

After this, Abraham's discouragement about not having an heir is recorded as is God's promise to him that his reward would be *"very great"* (Gen. 15:1). This is when God promised Abraham in no uncertain terms that Abraham would be a father—that *"your very own son shall be your heir"* (Gen. 15:4). Not only that, but his offspring would be innumerable as the stars of the heavens.

PAUL'S TEACHING FROM ABRAHAM'S EXPERIENCE

If Abraham had been like most of us—having a wife who was too old to have a baby—he would have said to God, "You cannot be serious! Do you expect me to believe *that*? Don't tease me." It seemed too good to be true. But, as D. L. Moody said, "No promise of God is too good to be true."

Abraham indeed *believed* it, and something more followed as a result: God counted Abraham's faith as *"righteousness"* (Gen. 15:6).

This event became Paul's "exhibit A" for his teaching of justification by faith. Paul made it clear that righteousness is *imputed* to the believer of the gospel. It is not imparted righteousness but rather *the way God sees* the person who believes. It is forensic, the way God regards us from a legal point of view. Imputed righteousness, then, is not in itself an emotional feeling; it is the way God judges the person who believes the promise. However, the work of the Holy Spirit that *enables* one to believe also gives one a measure of assurance of their being saved. A certain degree of assurance is of the essence of faith, namely, *"the assurance of things hoped for, the conviction of things not seen"* (Heb. 11:1). To put it another way, "infallible assurance," as the

Westminster Confession put it, is not of the essence of faith, but a measure of assurance is. A person knows whether he or she believes in their *heart*. The heart is the seat of faith. That said, it does not take great faith to be saved, but faith in a great Savior!

Although imputed righteousness is not an emotional feeling, it set Martin Luther (1483–1546) on fire! When Luther saw for himself that Paul's statement of justification by faith in Galatians and Romans meant *sola fide*—faith alone—Luther proceeded on his journey, which eventually turned Europe and Western civilization upside down. I wrote my book *Whatever Happened to the Gospel?* (Charisma House) in celebration of the five-hundredth anniversary of Luther's nailing his 95 Theses to the Wittenberg, Germany, church door on October 31, 1517. When someone asked me what I regarded as my greatest accomplishment in life, the answer was and is standing by the Wittenberg door before cameras and preaching the gospel to the world. My message was carried by TBN USA and TBN UK.

Why did Abraham believe it? Why does anyone believe it to this day? It is because of the sheer grace of God. It is His enabling grace: *"by grace ... through faith, ... not of works, lest anyone should boast"* (Eph. 2:8-9 NKJV). Paul raised the question *"Then what becomes of our boasting?"* He answered his own question: *"It is excluded"* (Rom. 3:27)! In other words, we can never brag about what *we* have done; it is something *God* has done. He is a jealous God; He gets all the glory.

After Abraham's faith was counted for righteousness, God continued to promise Abraham that the land of Canaan was to be Abraham's to possess (see Gen. 15:7). Canaan was not his native land. Abraham wanted further assurance about possessing the land. There followed instructions from God regarding a heifer, a goat, a dove, and a pigeon being sacrificed (see Gen. 15:8ff). This shows that the sacrifice of blood would be tied to God's promises. As for justification by faith alone, we *"are justified by his grace as a gift, through the redemption that is in Christ Jesus, whom God put forward as a propitiation by his blood, to be received by faith. This is to show God's righteousness, because in his divine forbearance he had passed over former sins. It was to show his righteousness at the present time, so that he might be just and the justifier of the one who has faith in Jesus"* (Romans 3:24-26).

The word *propitiation* means turning God's wrath away. The blood of Jesus satisfies the justice and wrath of God.

God told Abraham that his seed would be under affliction in Egypt—*"a land that is not theirs"*—where they would be afflicted for four hundred years then return to Canaan (Gen. 15:13-16). God repeated the promise again in Genesis 15:17-21. This is why Joseph, prime minister of Egypt, could say to his eleven brothers, who were overcome with guilt over betraying him, *"It was not you who sent me here, but God"* (Gen. 45:8). Although it would be a good while, the children of Israel eventually returned to Canaan under the leadership of Moses. This was initially promised to Abraham. Moses took Joseph's bones with him when the children of Israel returned to Canaan (see Exod. 13:19).

THE PROMISE AND THE OATH

For a good while God would renew the same old promise. Promises, promises. But, as we will see later, one day God would swear an oath to Abraham (see Heb. 6:17-18)! The inescapable truth about God's promises is that we tend to doubt after a while. The oath—which is infallible assurance—would eclipse the promise and leave no room for doubting. But the oath would wait a while before it came to Abraham—more than twenty years after his faith was counted as righteousness. It would be sworn by God *after* Isaac came—the promised child whom God had in mind all along—to Abraham (see Gen. 22:16-18).

Abraham began to doubt the promise of an heir who would come from his own body. His wife, Sarah, had a solution: Abraham should sleep with her servant Hagar. Abraham went along with the idea (see Gen. 16:1-2). It was not a good idea. But strange as it may seem, God also was at the bottom of it. And yet it was simultaneously to teach a lesson to demonstrate that Abraham and Sarah should not try to make things happen! They *did* believe the promise. But they jumped the gun and thought they were supposed to help God out! They wanted to make good the promise.

Having a child by Hagar was not Abraham's idea. It was Sarah's. Abraham assumed from the beginning that Sarah would be the mother of the promised child. That is partly what makes his faith so beautiful; he assumed that his seventy-year-old wife would be the mother of the promised child. Abraham would not have dreamed that Sarah would actually be ninety when the promised child finally came!

So after a while, Abraham began to doubt God's word that he would be a father. Then came Sarah's solution. Abraham slept with Hagar. Hagar conceived. But Sarah then got angry and turned against Abraham! And yet Abraham acquiesced to Sarah and offered to do whatever she wanted. Hagar consequently became afraid of Sarah and fled (see Gen. 16:3-6).

It is at this stage we discover that God was in it all. The angel of the Lord stepped in and even gave the embryonic child his name while still in Hagar's womb. Speaking to Hagar, the angel said:

> *Behold, you are pregnant and shall bear a son. You shall call his name Ishmael, because the Lord has listened to your affliction. He shall be a wild donkey of a man, his hand against everyone and everyone's hand against him, and he shall dwell over against all his kinsmen* (Genesis 16:11-12).

One of the most moving lines in all Holy Writ are these—the words of Hagar (of all people): *"You are a God of seeing"* (Gen. 16:13). This reads *"Thou God seest me"* in the King James Version.

It is an example of how God reaches out to the underdog. It shows how God cares about those no one would ever suspect to be chosen by God. Hagar added, *"Truly here I have seen him who looks after me"* (Gen. 16:13). The God of Abraham had blessed the unlikely Hagar.

In my book *Jonah* (Hodder & Stoughton), I state that Jonah, paradoxically as it may seem, was "out of the will of God in the will of God." In much the same way, God was not surprised with Abraham sleeping with Hagar. Ishmael's birth and Abraham's perception that Ishmael was the promised child were in the will of God although Ishmael was not the promised child. I also say that the charismatic movement was raised up of God. Like it or not, God's ways are higher than our ways; His thoughts higher than our thoughts (see Isa. 55:8-9).

ABRAHAM'S UNDERSTANDABLE ASSUMPTION

Yes, God was involved in Abraham's and Sarah's running ahead of the Lord. God had a plan for Ishmael. And the other thing we must never forget: *Abraham loved his firstborn, Ishmael.*

For over thirteen years Abraham assumed that Ishmael was *the* promised son. It is true that Abraham assumed Sarah would be the mother. It is also true that it was Sarah's idea that Abraham could sleep with Hagar and thus make the promise good. Furthermore, if Hagar had had a daughter rather than a son, that would have nullified the entire idea. But it was a son from Abraham's body. Ishmael's birth still fit the promise. After all these years, any doubt Abraham may have had about his son Ishmael being the promised son was long gone.

In other words, Abraham truly believed that Ishmael was the promised son. Likewise, many sincere and zealous people in the charismatic movement began to believe that this movement was God's final fulfilled promise to the Church before the end.

But one day Abraham—deeply devoted to Ishmael—was to receive a very unpleasant surprise. God stepped in with news that would have been fantastic news at one time: Sarah will conceive. If only God had said this immediately following the moment that Abraham's faith counted for righteousness! But God's ways are higher than our ways (see Isa. 55:9). Had a word like that come to Abraham several years before, Abraham would have been the happiest man on the earth. There was *no possible way* that the news twenty years before—that

Sarah would get pregnant—would have made Abraham unhappy. If only such a word had come from God many years before.

ABRAHAM'S WILLINGNESS TO CHANGE HIS MIND

But we now learn—when Ishmael was almost fourteen years old—that the news about Sarah having a baby boy did not thrill Abraham. But quite the opposite, as recorded in Genesis 17. And yet the manner in which God revealed the stunning news came to Abraham in a vision in several stages during which Abraham fell on his face: (1) that God is *"God Almighty"*; (2) that Abraham is to walk in holiness—to *"be blameless"*; (3) that God's *"covenant"* is mentioned; (4) that his name would *"be Abraham"* not Abram; and (5) that future male offspring at the age of *"eight days old"* would be required to be circumcised (Gen. 17:1-2, 10-13).

What God was now revealing was unprecedented in the life of Abraham. Keep in mind that God had already imputed righteousness to Abraham and promised him the land of Canaan some fourteen years before the emergence of the covenant of circumcision. This was very important to the apostle Paul in unfolding the doctrine of justification by faith. Paul emphasized strongly that Abraham was declared righteous *before* he was circumcised (see Rom. 4:10).

The word *covenant* is a translation of the Hebrew *berith*. It was an agreement between two partners who make binding promises to each other. When God brought in the covenant to Abraham—having already been counted as righteous—it meant that Abraham would get to experience God at a new and higher level. First, there came the revelation of a covenant between God and Abraham:

> *When Abram was ninety-nine years old the Lord appeared to Abram and said to him, "I am God Almighty; walk before me, and be blameless, that I may make my covenant between me and you, and may multiply you greatly"* (Genesis 17:1-2).

This covenant was initiated by God. As we saw above, God referred to Himself as *God Almighty* and added the command regarding holy living. The covenant would be between God and Abraham, and from that would come the multiplication of Abraham's seed. The word *berith* comes from a root word that means "cutting"—cutting of flesh. It brought blood. Hence the covenant of circumcision, the cutting of the male foreskin, was a *sign* of the covenant between God and Abraham (see Gen. 17:11). By agreeing to circumcision, Abraham demonstrated that he was keeping his end of the deal, that is, showing his faithfulness to God by personally being circumcised. Abraham himself at the age of ninety-nine was circumcised, as was Ishmael being thirteen (see Gen. 17:24-25).

THE PROMISE OF ISAAC WAS NOT GOOD NEWS AT FIRST

But in the same vision came the sobering news: Not only would Sarai be called Sarah, now ninety years old, but God said to a disappointed

Abraham, *"I will give you a son by her"* (Gen. 17:16). Indeed, from Sarah would come *"nations; kings of peoples* [came] *from her"* (Gen. 17:16).

When God appeared to Abraham earlier, Abraham fell on his face—apparently in worship. This time he *"fell on his face and laughed and said to himself, 'Shall a child be born to a man who is a hundred years old? Shall Sarah, who is ninety years old, bear a child?'"* (Gen. 17:17).

This is when we discover that Abraham was not a happy man. He pleaded: *"Oh that Ishmael might live before you!"* (Gen. 17:18).

If I may return to the general thesis of this book, I now refer to a conversation I had with a prominent charismatic leader on October 14, 1992—two days before my address at the previously mentioned Wembley Conference Centre. I would see his reaction as a litmus test. I asked him, "If you were to guess whether the charismatic movement is Ishmael or Isaac, which would you choose?"

He replied, "Isaac."

Knowing what I had planned to say the next day, I then said, "What if I were to tell you that I believe that the charismatic movement is Ishmael?"

He said in a quick second, "I hope not."

That is when I first began to think that my address would not be as popular as I hoped.

His reaction to the thought that the charismatic movement is not the ultimate work of God on the earth was similar to that of Abraham. After all he went through (e.g., sleeping with Hagar to make the promise good), Abraham now wanted the promised son to be Ishmael. He had made the adjustment to Ishmael, even though the mother was Hagar. He paid the price for Ishmael, having deep marital problems with Sarah over Hagar being pregnant. He loved Ishmael, having enjoyed this son for thirteen years. *"Oh that Ishmael might live before you. Please, Lord, let it be Ishmael."*

But no. As God's ways are higher than our ways, his thoughts higher than our thoughts, so too God had a different plan—for Ishmael, Abraham, and Sarah. Abraham then had to adjust to the promise of Isaac. God gave Ishmael his name; likewise, *"Sarah your wife shall bear you a son, and you shall call his name Isaac"* (Gen. 17:19). *Isaac* means "he laughs."

But Jesus answered them [the Sadducees], "You are wrong, because you know neither the Scriptures nor the power of God."
—Matthew 22:29

When the Word and the Spirit come together, there will be the biggest move of the Holy Spirit that the nations, and indeed, the world have ever seen.
—Smith Wigglesworth (1859–1947)

Chapter Three

THE WORD AND SPIRIT

The Word and the Spirit came together in the book of Acts: Word—*logos*—in classical Greek meant "faculty of thought or reason." Which comes first in order—the Word or the Spirit? It was the word of Jesus that told His followers to *"tarry"*—*"wait"*—in Jerusalem until they were clothed with power (Luke 24:49; Acts 1:4). You could say that the Word comes first in order. But on the Day of Pentecost (fifty days after Passover), the Spirit came in power:

> *Suddenly there came from heaven a sound like a mighty rushing wind, and it filled the entire house where they were sitting. And divided tongues as of fire appeared to them and rested on each one of them. And they were all filled with the Holy Spirit and began to speak in other tongues as the Spirit gave them utterance* (Acts 2:2-4).

Peter stood up to explain to curious Jews what had happened. The same Peter who cowardly denied knowing Jesus just a few weeks before now spoke with confidence, boldness, and utter fearlessness. He explained the amazing phenomenon that got everybody's attention—people speaking in other languages and understanding foreign words in their own language—was a fulfillment of Old Testament prophecies. Peter quoted from the prophet Joel, then applied the word to the person of Jesus who had recently been crucified by the Jews (see Joel 2:28-32). Peter said that all went according to *the definite plan and foreknowledge of God"* (Acts 2:23). He then quoted the words of David from Psalm 16 and Psalm 110 (see Acts 2:25-35). Such power accompanied Peter's words that hostile Jews were now *"cut to the heart"* and became compliant and begged to know, *"What shall we do?"* (Acts 2:37). Peter told them, *"Repent and be baptized every one of you in the name of Jesus Christ for the forgiveness of your sins, and you will receive the gift of the Holy Spirit"* (Acts 2:38). Three thousand were baptized (see Acts 2:41).

This was the first time, as far as I can tell, that the Word and Spirit came together at the same time. One could make the case that all that Jesus ever did was simultaneously the Word and Spirit at work. *"The words that I have spoken to you,"* said Jesus, *"are spirit and life"* (John 6:63). One could make the case that the ministry of Moses—and Elijah—was Word and Spirit ministry. In any case, it was the biblical preaching of Peter accompanied with Holy Spirit power that explains the initial success of the earliest church. The word *church* comes from *ecclesia*—meaning "the called out," referring to people, not a building.

Peter continued to minister in power. Joined by John, a forty-year-old man who had never walked was miraculously healed. It gave the Jerusalem church a platform. Most of the converts on the Day of Pentecost were from outside Jerusalem. Instead of allowing the crowds to focus on Peter and John, they used the occasion to preach the gospel (see Acts 3:12ff). The number of the converts *"came to about five thousand"* (Acts 4:4). The more the early church was persecuted, the more power it had. The people prayed aloud simultaneously, and not only was the place where they prayed *"shaken,"* but they were filled again with the Holy Spirit (Acts 4:31). It shows that being filled with the Spirit can be repeated. When Ananias and Sapphira lied about the money they took in from the property they sold, Peter saw through them. The husband and wife were both struck dead by the Holy Spirit (see Acts 5:1-11). People who wanted to be healed tried just to get in Peter's shadow (see Acts 5:15).

ISAAC AND A NEW LEVEL OF POWER

You may ask whether I believe this level of power will come with the coming of Isaac. I answer yes. Imagine the glory it will bring to God when the Church in our time demonstrates power like this! All this will be done while Jesus is seated on His throne at the right hand of God.

The conversion of Saul of Tarsus was a demonstration of the Word and Spirit. On his way to kill Christians, Saul was knocked to the ground by the Spirit. Jesus Himself spoke to Saul, and Saul, who later became known as Paul, became willing to do whatever Jesus ordered (see Acts 9:1-9). I fully expect that the next move of God will result in the conversion of surprising and most unlikely people—fierce God-haters, politicians, tramps, Muslims, Jews, billionaires, and movie stars.

Paul was a Word and Spirit man. It was he who articulated the teaching of justification by faith. He taught all over the Mediterranean area, founding churches in Corinth, Ephesus, Galatia, Philippi, and Thessalonica. He healed a man who had been paralyzed (see Acts 14:10). He also raised a man from the dead (see Acts 20:10).

Paul said to the Thessalonians, *"Our gospel came to you not only in word, but also in power and in the Holy Spirit"* (1 Thess. 1:5). When Paul said that, he implied that he *could* have preached without power. Did Paul ever preach without power? I have no idea. But he might have.

I certainly have. If I am totally honest, I have preached many more times without power than the times I have preached with a measure of power. On the other hand, it is possible that I preached with power when I didn't "feel" it. I know what it is to feel I preached pitifully and with no power—only to discover later someone was converted. It is also possible I only imagined I preached with power because I felt good in preaching!

In Miletus, Paul addressed the elders of Ephesus who came to him there. He warned of *"fierce wolves"* coming to Ephesus, *"not sparing the flock,"* even saying *"from among your own selves"* would come men twisting things to get their own disciples (Acts 20:29-30). Some thirty years later, Jesus Himself addressed the church of Ephesus from the right hand of God. He complimented them for a number of things but noted that they had lost their first love (see Rev. 2:4). We can safely say that Ephesus was a Word and Spirit church at one time. But what did Jesus mean by their losing their first love? Was it their emphasis on the Word that diminished—or did Jesus mean a diminishing spiritually? Or zeal?

Paul reminded them that they were saved by "grace through faith" and not of works lest they boast (see Eph. 2:8-9). Paul had equally warned them about grieving the Spirit (see Eph. 4:30). He also urged them to *"be filled with the Spirit"* (Eph. 5:18). I cannot say for sure whether losing their first love was a theological backsliding—that is, of their upholding the gospel—or a spiritual backsliding—that is, their having a form of godliness without the power (as prophesied by Paul in 2 Timothy 3:1-9). I do know that scholarly studies on the "doctrines of grace in the apostolic fathers" (e.g., second-century teachers) have shown that Christian teaching appeared to indicate minimal under-standing of sovereign grace, but that Christianity had degenerated to mere morality. Indeed, it was not until the time of Athanasius (c. 296–373) and Augustine (354–430) that the Christian faith reflected the teachings of John and Paul.

There are churches today where people only anticipate a word. There are churches where people go to see—that is, to see a miracle. We saw some at Westminster Chapel. But people mostly came not to see but to hear. "Thank you for your word," they would say. That is what they came for; that is what they got. There are churches where people don't expect to hear much; they come to see. But, as Lyndon Bowring put it, when the Word and Spirit come together—when Isaac comes of age—those who come to see will hear, and those who come to hear will see.

A Silent Divorce

In my aforementioned address at the Wembley Conference Centre in 1992, I stated that there has been a "silent divorce" between the

Word and the Spirit in the Church, speaking generally. The reason I call it silent is that we don't know when it happened. Was it before the end of the first century? Was it when people like B. B. Warfield (1851–1921) brought in the teaching of cessationism? Cessationism is the theory that some people turned into a dogma, namely, a false teaching that claims that the gifts of the Spirit "ceased" after the first century. It is utterly without scriptural foundation. *"Jesus Christ is the same yesterday and today and forever"* (Heb. 13:8). Likewise, the Holy Spirit is the same yesterday and today and forever! The notion of cessationism—normative theology for some—quenches the Spirit before the Holy Spirit is welcomed!

In a divorce, sometimes the children stay with the mother; sometimes the children stay with the father. In this silent divorce, there have been those who are on the Word side and those who are on the Spirit side.

What is the difference? Word people say that the honor of God's name will not be restored until we get back to solid theology. We must earnestly *"contend for the faith ... once ... delivered to the saints"* (Jude 3). Word people say that we must get back to Bible preaching, knowing our doctrine such as justification by faith, assurance of salvation, and the sovereignty of God.

What is wrong with this emphasis? Absolutely nothing. It was the teaching of Paul, Peter, John, Athanasius, Augustine, the Reformers, and people like Jonathan Edwards.

Spirit people say that we must get back to the book of Acts where there were signs wonders and miracles, gifts of the Spirit in operation. Get in Peter's shadow, and you get healed. Lie to the Holy Spirit, and you are struck dead.

What is wrong with this emphasis on the Spirit? Absolutely nothing. It is what is truly needed.

There have been brief epochs in church history when the power of the Spirit in miracles was seen. I urge you to read Jack Deere's book *Surprised by the Power of the Spirit.* There is evidence that John Knox's (c. 1514–1572) son-in-law raised a man from the dead.

The Word and Spirit were revived in some measure during the Wesleyan and Whitefield revivals in the eighteenth century. The Holy Spirit was powerfully present during the Welsh revival of 1904–1905. Dr. Lloyd-Jones used to enthrall me with stories that came out of the Welsh revival. He described a man who worked in a coal mine and came home from work to find his wife had not prepared his supper but was at church in the height of the revival. The man was so angry that he decided to go to the church and bust up the meeting. When he arrived at the church, he could not get in because it was so crowded at the door. Nevertheless, he pushed people back and made his way inside the church. The next thing he remembered was being on his knees in front of the pulpit asking God to save him! People who witnessed the scene said he literally walked on the top of each pew from the back to the front and fell before the pulpit in the front of the church. And yet, strange as it may seem, there was minimal preaching during the Welsh revival. This gave some Reformed people ammunition to oppose the Welsh revival. Dr. Lloyd-Jones also shared with me that one pastor who had vehemently criticized the Welsh revival was struck with blindness soon afterward.

The Spirit was powerfully present in the Pentecostal movement. One should be afraid to criticize it. Many in the charismatic movement were undoubtedly touched by the raw power of God. One should be afraid to criticize it.

TODAY: OFTEN ONE OR THE OTHER

As for the Word and the Spirit today, the problem is, so it seems to me, wherever I travel in the world, it is one or the other! You have Word churches where the emphasis is on solid teaching. You have Spirit churches where the miraculous has actually taken place. But to find a church that is equally both nowadays is—in my honest view— extremely rare. There are some. But not many. The evidence of this, if I may refer to some things I shared in my book *Prophetic Integrity,* is that some of the most gifted men had minimal understanding of theology; they admitted to me that they did not read their Bibles! I would add that, to have prophetic fulfillment, as several of them truly had, is evidence of the power of God in them.

When I first met Paul Cain and discovered firsthand what gifting he had, I said to him, "Paul, you need my theology; I need your power."

His reply: "You have a deal."

That is when the notion of the Word and Spirit was borne in my own life—and his.

Jesus said that the Sadducees were ignorant of *both*—the Scriptures and the power of God. To say to the Sadducees that they were ignorant of the Scriptures was the supreme insult to them. They were people who fancied that they had the monopoly on Old Testament teaching.

The Sadducees had brought up a hypothetical illustration to Jesus, hoping to catch Him and vindicate their assumption that there is no life after death, no such thing as angels or a resurrection of the dead:

> *Teacher, Moses said, "If a man dies having no children, his brother must marry the widow and raise up offspring for his brother." Now there were seven brothers among us. The first married and died, and having no offspring left his wife to his brother. So too the second and the third, down to the seventh. After them all, the woman died. In the resurrection, therefore, of the seven, whose wife shall she be? For they all had her* (Matthew 22:24-28).

Jesus immediately gave this blunt assessment to the Sadducees regarding their teaching: *"You are wrong"* (Matt. 22:29). This would be like telling a cessationist that he does not know the Bible! And Jesus quoted the very verse that every person in Israel knew (or thought they knew) backward and forward: *"Have you not read ... 'I am the God of Abraham, and the God of Isaac, and the God of Jacob'?"* (Matt. 22:31). This would be like one saying to any Bible believer, "Have you never read John 3:16?" And yet Jesus in one stroke turned their teaching on its head when He showed that God *"is not the God of the dead, but of the living"*—quoting Exodus 3:6 (Matt. 22:32). Exodus 3:6, when truly understood, shows that Abraham was still alive and well! Isaac is still living! Jacob is very much alive! That understanding of Exodus 3:6 had not once entered their minds! Jesus *"silenced the Sadducees"* (Matt. 22:34). Indeed, the crowd was *"astonished at his teaching"* (Matt. 22:33).

We might observe three things at this point. First, the word translated *astonished* (Gr. *exeplessonto*) is the same word used when people observed a miracle performed by Jesus (see Matt. 22:33; Mark 7:37). It shows that Jesus can astonish people by His *Word* as easily as He can astonish by a *miracle*. Second, I suspect many of us imagine that only a healing miracle is capable of astonishing people today. And yet I predict that the coming wave of the Spirit will show revelation of words in the Bible that will dazzle people as much as any miracle could. Third, as the hymn that was based on Pastor John Robinson's (1575–1625) word to the Pilgrim Fathers at Plymouth, England, in 1620 put it, "The Lord hath yet more light and truth / To break forth from His Word" (George Rawson 1807–1689).

It is noteworthy that the word *know*—in that the Sadducees did not *know* the Scriptures or the power of God—is the Greek word *oida*—meaning *knowledge of a well-known fact.* In other words, the Sadducees should have readily understood the salient meaning of Exodus 3:6. The same was true regarding the power of God. The Sadducees never intended to talk about God's power—of which they knew singularly nothing. But Jesus brought up the subject of God's power. Jesus' reply to the Sadducees shows that He believed that one should be acquainted with *both*: the Scriptures *and* the power of God.

The Sadducees knew neither. With most of us today, we seem to emphasize one or the other.

It is surely true that, when the Word is joined by the Spirit in great measure, the simultaneous combination will mean spontaneous combustion and bring the awakening that we need so desperately.

WHAT IS MEANT BY "WORD"?

On the day following my address at Wembley, I received a phone call from a prominent Christian leader in London. He was one of the few who did accept my view but had an urgent question. He asked, "By 'Word,' R. T., do you mean Reformed teaching?" Good question.

I knew what this man meant by Reformed teaching. But not all readers will know what this is. I will be brief and as simple as possible in a few sentences. Since the sixteenth century, Protestantism has been generally divided between two theological perspectives: Calvinism—stressing predestination and eternal security of the believer; and Arminianism—stressing free will and the possibility you can lose your salvation. Calvinism, named for John Calvin (1509–1564), is Reformed teaching. It is my own position. I have no desire to convert the reader to my position. But the aforementioned man who phoned me the morning after I gave my address at Wembley Conference Centre knew that I am Reformed. That is why he wondered if I narrowed the "Word" to Reformed teaching. In short: by Word and Spirit did I mean that "Word" must necessarily be Calvinistic? Answer: no.

You can be an Arminian like John Wesley and believe everything I teach in this book. I remember that Dr. Martyn Lloyd-Jones, a staunch Calvinist, affirmed John Wesley (1703–1791)—an Arminian—as a true man of God. Dr. Lloyd-Jones got more support and ammunition from Wesley for his view of the baptism of the Holy Spirit than he got from most Calvinists! I say that, if Dr. Lloyd-Jones could embrace the John Wesleys of this world, so can I. John Wesley also said his theology was "within a hair's breadth of Calvinism."

Martyn Lloyd-Jones always described himself as a "Calvinistic Methodist." He was enamored with Wesley's view of the Holy Spirit—that one "feels" something—namely the immediate and direct witness of the Spirit when the Spirit is received. Regarding Galatians 3, Lloyd-Jones observed that one could not "receive" the Spirit if he did not know when the Spirit came. Look at the content of Charles Wesley's (1707–1788) hymns!

In a word, I believe the Word and Spirit together means that you can have solid theology without dotting all the i's or crossing all the t's of what some call orthodoxy.

However, here is what I suspect to be the minimum to qualify for the Word and Spirit to come together: either the belief in the Nicene Creed or the Apostles' Creed. I would add to that one must have the conviction that all people need to be saved. The "Word" is sufficiently contained in either of the following creeds.

Here is the Nicene Creed (AD 325):

> I believe in one God,
> the Father almighty,
> maker of heaven and earth,
> of all things visible and invisible.
> And in one Lord Jesus Christ,
> the Only Begotten Son of God,
> born of the Father before all ages.
> God from God, Light from Light,
> true God from true God,

begotten, not made,

consubstantial with the Father;

through him all things were made.

For us men and for our salvation

he came down from heaven,

and by the Holy Spirit

was incarnate of the Virgin Mary,

and became man.

For our sake

he was crucified under Pontius Pilate,

he suffered death and was buried,

and rose again on the third day

in accordance with the Scriptures.

He ascended into heaven and is seated

at the right hand of the Father.

He will come again in glory

to judge the living and the dead

and his kingdom will have no end.

And in the Holy Spirit, the Lord,

the giver of life, who proceeds

from the Father and the Son,

who with the Father and the Son

is adored and glorified,

who has spoken through the prophets.

And one, holy, catholic*

and apostolic** Church.

I confess one baptism

for the forgiveness of sins

and I look forward to the resurrection

of the dead

and the life of the world to come. Amen.

*Catholic means universal.
**Apostolic means the writings of the apostles of Jesus.

Here is the Apostles' Creed (written between AD 340 and AD 700):

I believe in God, the Father almighty,

creator of heaven and earth.

I believe in Jesus Christ, his only Son, our Lord,

who was conceived by the Holy Spirit

and born of the virgin Mary.

He suffered under Pontius Pilate,

was crucified, died, and was buried;

he descended to hell.

The third day he rose again from the dead.

He ascended to heaven

and is seated at the right hand of God the Father
almighty.

From there he will come to judge the living and the

dead.

I believe in the Holy Spirit,

the holy catholic* church,

the communion of saints,

the forgiveness of sins,

the resurrection of the body,

and the life everlasting. Amen.

*This means universal—the true Christian Church of all times and in all places.

In other words, I would not press a particular soteriology to be upheld. I personally believe in the Westminster Confession (1647). We can also have a sound doctrine of salvation and be "perfectly orthodox, perfectly useless," as Dr. Lloyd-Jones would say.

I can safely tell you what will be manifest in the next great move of God: that people are converted by the hundreds of thousands all over the world. Yes, it will be a restoration of the gospel, as in Romans 4. It will be in line with historic Christianity. But what will be more talked about will be a renewal of the fear of God. Of the need of righteousness in the land. An awareness that God is alive and in control. As it is put by Ezekiel, *"Then they will know that I am the Lord"* (Ezek. 6:14). And that Jesus is coming very soon.

And to the one who does not work but believes in him who justifies the ungodly, his faith is counted as righteousness.... No unbelief made him waver concerning the promise of God, but he grew strong in his faith as he gave glory to God, fully convinced that God was able to do what he had promised. That is why his faith was "counted to him as righteousness."
—Romans 4:5, 20-22

The Bible teaches justification by faith alone, and yet ultimately there is only one way anybody is saved in the presence of God, and that is through works. The question is not whether we are going to be saved through works, the question is whose works. We are saved through the works of One who fulfilled the terms of the covenant of works. That is why it is not just the death of Christ that redeems us, but it is also the life of Christ.
—R. C. Sproul (1939–2017)

The key to the next great move of God on the earth is the book of Romans and especially Romans 4.
—John Paul Jackson (1950–2015)

Chapter Four

ROMANS 4

In my book *The Anointing* (Charisma House), I referred to two men who had a major influence on me—Martyn Lloyd-Jones and Paul Cain, two men most unlikely to be linked together! You could say that they were polar opposites in some ways. The same would certainly be true of R. C. Sproul and John Paul Jackson. I only met R. C. Sproul once, however, but his statement I quoted above sums up my own understanding of the book of Romans and especially Romans 4. The quote of John Paul Jackson is taken from the words of the messenger of God, which I shall pass on below.

Romans 4 may be understood in two parts: The first half unveils the truth of justification by faith alone (Rom. 4:1-12); the second half shows the principle of inheritance by persistent faith (Rom. 4:13-25). The first part of Romans 4 refers to Abraham's faith in Genesis 15:5-6—which is Paul's Exhibit A for his teaching of justification by faith alone. The second part of Romans 4 also refers to Abraham's life but after he was circumcised in Genesis 17. This is when he was told that Ishmael was *not* the promised son, but that Sarah would have a son—who would be called Isaac.

In short, the first half of Romans 4 shows how we are saved; the second part of Romans 4 shows how believers are called to come into their inheritance. All people are saved the same way—by believing God's promise; all believers come into their inheritance the same way—by persistent faith.

John Paul's Vision

John Paul Jackson came to see me at Westminster Chapel in September 2001. He had a word for me. He wanted to share a vision he had on November 27, 1986. When he first shared this, he spoke from memory. But he also wrote it out; these are his own words:

> I was in a large room in Heaven, much like a Temple setting. It was pure white in color. Everything was white. To my left were tall double doors, each about 20 ft. tall and totaling 20 ft. in width. So the total opening was 20 ft. x 20 ft. To my right were four rows of white stone like bleachers or rows of seats.
>
> I heard the doors open and watched as a line of men began to walk into the room, crossing in front of me toward the four rows of white stone. The first men who walked by were all well-known and some were internationally known. However, not all well-known preachers were there, but all who were there, in the front of the line, were. I did not know the men who came later in the line. The line was led by a well-known pastor who

led the men to fill the third row (next to the highest row). Once that row was full, the men then began to fill in the second row and then the first row. All those there stood as if waiting for something to happen. The men on the third row were so proud to be there, standing above the others. There was one well-known pastor/evangelist on the third row who was to the left of the center and was jockeying to take the center position. I was wondering why no one was standing on the top or fourth row, which was empty.

A tall, fiery white-haired messenger, with piercing green-blue eyes, came walking in, and he suddenly appeared on this high podium as if he were translated there. It was the highest thing in the room, and the fiery messenger stood looking down at the rows of men. He opened the Bible and said, with a commanding voice, "Gentlemen, I have a word for you and the Body of Christ from the Throne Room of God concerning the next great move of God in the earth. The key to this move of God is found in the Bible, in the book of Romans, and in particular Romans chapter 4."

He said, "This word is contained within the whole of the Scripture, but it is an unseen truth. The key is unseen, due to the current doctrines of the church. This truth is so hard to embrace and attain that it is not even considered by most." He went on to say, "This truth will mark the church in the coming move of God, and it will separate and distinguish the coming church from the present church." He then began to unveil this truth for what seemed to be a long period of time, but

I do not remember what he said about those things. As I returned, it was removed from my memory, as if I was not the one to proclaim the fullness of it.

The messenger then looked around and said once again, "This message is from the Throne Room of God concerning the next great move of God on the earth. The secret to this move of God is found in the book of Romans and Romans 4 in particular. But you men on the third row have already violated the Romans 4 principles. None of your ministries will grow, many will languish, and some of you will die without fulfilling your purpose. However, you men on the second row and first row, if you do not violate the Romans 4 principles—in a day you think not, in a day you think least likely—the Lord will suddenly catapult you over those who currently lord their ministries over you to the fourth row where no one has stood since the early church."

The men on the third row began to protest and argue with the messenger, but He would not argue with them. It was as if what was said was said.

That is the end of the vision.

MY REACTION

What made me feel that this vision had a ring of authenticity was the reference to the book of Romans generally and Romans 4 specifically.

I immediately thought to myself, and said to John Paul, "People today do not appreciate Romans. I am amazed that you, John Paul, have come up with this. It is very neglected. Romans 4 is about the gospel—justification by faith alone—what Luther and the Reformers taught. This would mean that the next great move of God will be characterized by a restoration of the gospel!" What was even more interesting is that John Paul admitted that he himself did not know what Romans 4 was about. This suggests to me that he couldn't have made this up or even thought of it!

Romans 4 was in fact at the heart of Martin Luther's discovery in the sixteenth century, which turned the Western world upside down. It is what Jonathan Edwards preached in Northampton, Massachusetts, from 1733–1738 as the New England Awakening was reaching its zenith. Edwards wrote that during that time "the whole town was filled with the talk of God." John Wesley had grasped the teaching of justification by faith before Whitefield did and actually taught it to George Whitefield (1714–1770).

After having that vision, John Paul of course read and studied Romans 4 many times. When he read the first edition of the book *Word and Spirit* by Paul Cain and me—which included my address on Ishmael and Isaac—he said he cried as he read my reference to Romans 4 because he had never read anyone or heard anybody who referred to Romans 4. I will add that what gripped me most about Romans 4 was the teaching of the gospel; what gripped John Paul was the implication of the miraculous—that Abraham at almost age one hundred and Sarah around ninety would have a son. To John Paul, then, the next great move of God will be characterized by miracles.

What made *me* feel most comfortable about John Paul's vision, then, was that the "next great move of God," assuming the vision was absolutely authentic, meant that the historic Christian faith would be central again. There is a continuity of understanding and similarity from the teaching of the apostles to Saint Augustine, Athanasius, Luther, Calvin, Edwards, Whitefield, Wesley, and C. H. Spurgeon. It is a far cry from what is popular today—"what's in it for me" and "feel good" teaching. And if it also meant that apostolic power would be given to preachers today to stand where no one has stood since the days of the early church, then it would mean that the combination of Word and Spirit coming together simultaneously as seen in the book of Acts would be observed by all.

These things said, the second part of Romans 4 would, therefore, have equal relevance. It refers to Abraham having not only imputed righteousness but also personal righteousness. In other words, he would demonstrate true godliness and a robust faith that Sarah would have a son. That was part of Abraham's own inheritance. The teaching of inheritance—as seen in Romans 4 and the Epistle to the Hebrews—is barely known, hardly taught, almost entirely overlooked, and therefore unappreciated. You may recall that the messenger of God in John Paul's vision said it was an "unseen truth."

I do indeed suspect that the truth of Romans 4 is largely unseen and unknown nowadays. The apostle Paul also referred to calling into existence *"things that do not exist"* (Rom. 4:17). This would indeed mean seeing undoubted healings and miracles. In my conversations with John Paul about Romans 4, which we had often, the main thing that he himself was most excited about was the promise of miracles as seen in the latter part of Romans 4: Abraham believing that Sarah would have a son. What gripped me most, however, was the promise of the gospel being restored. John Paul told me repeatedly that the next great move of God would include people being raised from the dead.

One other thing I must add: The teaching of cessationism will perish overnight.

You may also recall the words of John Paul as stated above in what he wrote out, "As if I was not the one to proclaim the fullness of it"; this could be seen as a cryptic reference to his own untimely death. John Paul was 36 when he had the vision in 1986. He was only 65 when he died in 2015.

I will now elaborate on the two parts of Romans 4.

IMPUTED RIGHTEOUSNESS

The word *impute* means "to credit." The Greek word is *logizetai*—"reckoned," "imputed," or "credited with." It is a free gift. If you *embrace the promise* in the gospel—that Jesus Christ died for your sin—His righteousness is imputed to you; that is, you are *treated by God as if His righteousness were yours*. It is put to your credit. You are reckoned by God Himself to be righteous. This comes by faith, trust, relying on the promise.

This means you will go to Heaven and not to hell when you die. You have been *"justified by his blood"* and saved from the *"wrath of God"* (Rom. 5:9). I'm sorry, but seldom does one hear preaching nowadays on the wrath of God. Since people don't like to hear it, preachers accommodate by not getting around to preaching it.

There are actually three "causes" that lie behind anyone being justified by faith.

First, the meritorious cause. This is the life, death, resurrection, and intercession of Jesus. By life, I mean the perfect life He lived. He kept the law for us. His parents had Him circumcised according to the law (see Luke 2:21). He was even baptized for us—*"to fulfill all righteousness,"* He said to John the Baptist (Matt. 3:15). He had perfect faith for us, which is why Paul said that if we believe "in" Christ, then we would be justified by the faith "of" Christ (see Gal. 2:20 KJV). Jesus promised to fulfill the law and to finish the work God called Him to do (see Matt. 5:17; John 4:34). He did it (see John 19:30). By death is meant His blood (see Rom. 3:25; 5:9). He was raised for our justification (see Rom. 3:25). He ever lives to intercede for us (see Heb. 7:25). He intercedes with a perfect faith so that Paul could say, *"I live by the faith of the Son of God"* (Gal. 2:20 KJV).

This, then, is the meritorious cause of our justification. Our faith in and by itself is not what saves us; it is the object of our faith.

Second, the efficient cause. What *enables* a person to believe? Since not all have faith and all are born *"dead"* in trespasses and sins, what makes the difference (Eph. 2:1; 2 Thess. 3:2)? The answer is the Holy Spirit. He "quickens"—gives life. No one "can" come to the Father unless he be drawn (John 6:44). It is the Holy Spirit that enables a person to rely on Christ alone.

Third, the instrumental cause. That is when we consciously transfer our trust in good works to the work of Jesus. The gospel must be *believed.* All that Jesus did for us by His life and death is of no value until we believe. That is the message of John 3:16—whoever *"believes"* on the Son has eternal life.

This is the meaning of *"faith to faith"* in Romans 1:17: In the gospel is *"a righteousness from God"* that is revealed *"from faith to faith"*—the faith of Christ and our faith. The faith of Christ in providing the meritorious cause must be ratified by our faith—or we will not be saved. It is the faith of Jesus joined by our faith that gives us an imputed righteousness.

It is the imputed righteousness of Christ that gets us to Heaven, not our own righteousness. As the hymn "My Hope Is Built on Nothing Less" affirms:

> My hope is built on nothing less than Jesus' blood
> and righteousness;
>
> I dare not trust the sweetest frame, but wholly lean
> on Jesus' Name.
>
> When He shall come with trumpet sound, O may I
> then in Him be found,
>
> Dressed in His righteousness alone, faultless to stand
> before the throne.

> —**Edward Mote** (1797–1874)

The instrumental cause—our faith—is conscious. But imputed righteousness is not a feeling. It is *what God does* when you believe that your only hope of going to Heaven is His blood.

You may not *feel* righteous. Someone may say, "You don't look righteous to me." You might even feel ridiculous—to think that God sees you as righteous merely because you believe the gospel. Indeed, it may make you feel utterly unworthy. Dr. Martyn Lloyd-Jones used to say that a Christian is someone who is "surprised" that he or she is a Christian!

It is not a feeling, then. It is the way God sees you. It is legal. Forensic. It is what is declared in Heaven. It is the way a most holy God regards you. When you trust His Word, He regards you as totally righteous because the righteousness of His Son has been put to your credit. When Abraham believed the promise that his seed would be as the sand of the sea, though he was eighty years old and his wife was past the age of having children, God declared him to be a righteous man. He had been a sun worshipper. He had no background that would endear him to the true God. He had no good works to show. That is Paul's main point in the first half of Romans 4.

This teaching is not always easy to understand for many of us— even harder to believe! Not everybody can take it in. At least at first. It took Martin Luther some four years—1513–1515—to understand it. It seemed too good to be true. He referred to his breakthrough as his "tower experience." This phrase has a double meaning. First, Luther studied in a tower near the church in Wittenberg, Germany. It stands there today. I have seen it. Second, when he had his breakthrough, it was equally a "tower experience" because of what it did for him. It set him free. He was set on fire and changed the world. When he saw what was described above—that faith means *fide sola*, "faith only," and that Paul literally means "faith without works" in Romans 1:17— he became fearless.

For in it [the gospel] *the righteousness of God is revealed from faith to* [Gr. eis] *faith, as it is written, "the righteous shall live by faith"* (Romans 1:17).

The freedom from the gospel that made Luther fearless will make you fearless, too. If you have not had this explained to you before, and you see this for the first time for yourself, congratulations! It will turn your world upside down!

Most of my preaching during the last twenty years—all over the world—has been largely to Charismatics. Not all have been Charismatics, but many have been. I have been shocked how few Charismatics, especially in America, have understood and embraced this teaching. I don't mean to be unfair, but a large percentage of Charismatics I have preached to have (apparently) had little if any teaching of the true gospel. Or it had not sunk in. You may ask, how do you know that? I answer, because when I present the gospel and ask people to stand who have been trusting in something other than the death of Jesus, a large percentage almost always stand.

I am not saying that all those who stood to confess Christ unashamedly were not saved. Many undoubtedly were following the Lord with sincere hearts, and the fact that they readily stood when I would give the invitation shows me that their hearts were eager to show their faith. I do not believe you have to be theologically sound to be saved. In fact, I think you could be theologically sound and be lost! I think you might be theologically short of the theology of Romans—as long as you believe that Jesus is God and rose from the dead—and be saved.

I'm sorry, but many Christians I have preached to in the last twenty years believe they get to Heaven by being good enough. When I ask the question "If you stood before God and He were to ask you, 'Why should I let you into My Heaven?'" too many answer by saying honestly, "I have tried to live a good life." Or something akin to good works or being faithful. People by nature cannot get it out of their heads that we get to Heaven *entirely* by what Jesus did for us.

This is why I was astounded—thrilled—by John Paul's vision. It would not have come from a Reformed person. This is because most Reformed people don't have (or believe in) visions. It came from John Paul Jackson, of all people—greatly loved and admired by Charismatics and Pentecostals.

FAITH ALONE IN CHRIST ALONE

How can faith without works justify us? The answer is, God can reckon us righteous because His justice has been satisfied by the blood of Jesus—fully satisfied. When Jesus was dying and shedding His precious blood, that blood was crying out for justice. God's justice was satisfied, as these lyrics from "In Christ Alone" attest:

> In Christ alone my hope is found
> He is my light, my strength, my song
> On that cross as Jesus died
> The wrath of God was satisfied
> For every sin on Him was laid
> Here in the death of Christ I live
>
> **—Keith Getty and Stuart Townend**

Jesus paid it all. The words *"It is finished"* are the English translation for the Greek word *tetelestai* (John 19:30). *Tetelestai* was a colloquial expression in the ancient marketplace that meant "paid in full."

Jesus paid it all, all to Him I owe;
Sin has left a crimson stain;
He washed it white as snow.

—**Elvina M. Hall** (1820–1889)

Paul laid the groundwork for Romans 4 in Romans 3. He showed how God could be just and merciful at the same time: *"be just and the justifier of the one who has faith in Jesus"* (Gr. *pisteos Iesou*—faith *of* Jesus) (Rom. 3:26). It is because Jesus' blood was a *"propitiation"* for our sins (Rom. 3:25). *Propitiation* means "to turn the Father's wrath away."

From this, Paul taught that justification is by faith alone. Faith is the instrumental—and necessary—cause of our being justified. But no one can boast. No one can brag. No one can say, "Look at the wonderful thing I did." It is a work of the Spirit. Hence the question, what becomes of our boasting? The answer: *"It is excluded"* (Rom. 3:27). Such a person is humbled that he would have this glorious benefit. It is by the sheer grace of God.

If we are to believe that John Paul Jackson's vision is indeed from God, we have this to look forward to in the next great move of God.

But there is more in Romans 4 that needs to be examined. We turn to this now.

IMPARTED RIGHTEOUSNESS

If the first part of Romans 4 is largely neglected and misunderstood, the latter part of Romans 4 is probably even more so. It is indeed, I suspect, an "unseen" truth. If we are to take John Paul's vision seriously, one must note that the messenger of God added that the teaching of Romans 4 is hard to believe "due to the current doctrines of the church." Because it is hard to embrace, it is "not even considered by most." I would say then that this is true with regard to *both* parts of Romans 4. The first part—justification by faith "alone"—is not considered by most. Roman Catholicism rejected it. Protestantism generally does not uphold justification by faith alone. Pentecostals and Charismatics, in my experience with them, generally do not teach this. Nearly everyone wants to attach "works" to faith in order to guarantee one's justification. This is also why the book of James is misunderstood. It was even misunderstood by Martin Luther. People interpret James 2:14—*"Can that faith save him?"*—as the basis of one's salvation or assurance of salvation: that faith must have works to be saved. I will show below that James is not referring to assurance of salvation at all but to the effectiveness of one's testimony. James does not contradict Paul the slightest bit.

The second part of Romans 4 refers to Abraham accepting the truth that Sarah will have a son. You will recall that Abraham was told that his heir would be his own son—not his servant Eliezer. He believed the promise. He also naturally assumed that his heir would be Sarah's child. This promise regarding Abraham's seed also referred to the land (see Gen. 15:7-8). The promise, therefore, was twofold: (1) that the heir would be from Abraham's *own body,* and (2) his seed—innumerable as the grains of the sand of the sea—would inherit the *land.*

THE MYSTERY

Of course, God Himself *knew* that Abraham's son would *eventually* be Sarah's—not Hagar's—child! So why did God not allow Sarah to conceive when Abraham was eighty, when she was seventy, and not ninety? Why did God let Abraham think for nearly fourteen years that Ishmael was the promised child? You tell me! I can only answer with Isaiah 55:8-9: that God's ways are higher than our ways. His thoughts are not our thoughts; His ways are not our ways. Indeed, *"how inscrutable* [are] *his ways!"* said Paul (Rom. 11:33).

What we know is that Abraham's seed would one day be born not only in Canaan but the *"world"*; indeed, his offspring would reach *"many nations"* (Rom. 4:13, 17).

The amazing faith of Abraham to believe that Sarah at the age of ninety would have a baby would seem out of reach for most. I will admit that I find this very, very challenging if I am to repeat the equivalent of such faith. Am I to believe that I too must have faith that is the equivalent to Abraham believing that a man aged one hundred could produce a baby with a wife aged ninety? Paul regarded Abraham as *"the father of us all."* This means that we must follow Abraham in believing the double promise: (1) of the gospel of Jesus Christ, *and* (2) living a life of godliness that seems out of reach.

Please note that the promise of imputed righteousness as quoted in Romans 4:23 was not originally made to Abraham when he was nearly a hundred; it was when he was eighty. The words that righteousness was *"counted to him"* were not first said when he was nearly a hundred (Rom. 4:22); it was at age eighty to show that *the faith that Abraham had twenty years before had increased!* He *"grew strong in his faith"* (Rom. 4:20).

Are you and I not justified by faith until we have Abraham's faith when he was nearly a hundred? No! Abraham believed the promise when he was eighty. The equivalent, then, is that we believe the gospel. As Paul concluded in Romans 4, imputed righteousness is ours when we believe *"in him who raised from the dead Jesus our Lord, who was delivered up for our trespasses and raised for our justification"* (Rom. 4:24-25). We are saved not by the extraordinary faith Abraham had at the age of one hundred but at the simple faith he had when he was eighty: *"He believed the Lord, and he counted it to him as righteousness"* (Gen. 15:6). As Paul put it later in Romans, *"If you confess with your mouth that Jesus is Lord and believe in your heart that God raised him from the dead, you will be saved"* (Rom. 10:9).

That is what you and I are called to do.

INHERITANCE

But God is not finished with us when we are first converted. All Christians are called to come into their inheritance. Inheritance is a reward for obedience. Some Christians come into their inheritance and some don't (see 1 Cor. 3:14-15). For example, some will receive a reward at the judgment seat of Christ; some will forfeit a reward but will be saved by fire. Inheritance and reward may be used interchangeably (see Col. 3:24). Abraham came into his inheritance. God wants us to continue to follow in the steps of Abraham.

Possibly the best way to explain inheritance is to fast-forward to the time of Joshua. Understanding inheritance is key—essential—to understanding the boundaries given to the twelve nations of Israel after they conquered Canaan. What we know is that where each tribe would live, or possess, was utterly out of their hands. The boundaries—whether Judah, Dan, Asher, or Benjamin—were chosen by "lot." That way Joshua could not be accused of favoritism.

Likewise, it is God who chooses our inheritance: *"He chose our inheritance for us, the pride of Jacob, whom he loved"* (Ps. 47:4 NIV).

David could say, *"The lines have fallen for me in pleasant places; indeed, I have a beautiful inheritance"* (Ps. 16:6).

The first part of Romans 4, then, is about God *imputing* righteousness to those who believe the gospel; this is what saves us and makes us worthy of Heaven. It is not our righteousness but God's—the righteousness of Jesus—that saves us. The second part of Romans 4 is about sanctification. This is about God *imparting* righteousness to us: Sanctification comes by the help of the Holy Spirit. *To put it another way, salvation is what God does by the Holy Spirit; sanctification is what we do by the Holy Spirit.* It is a challenge. It is godliness. It is integrity. It is obedience. It is honoring God. It can be a struggle. It can be wrestling. It is fighting the devil. It is overcoming temptation. It is resisting the flesh.

When God told Abraham that Ishmael was not going to be the promised son, it was hard news. But even more challenging news was that Abraham was required to believe that Sarah at the age of ninety would conceive. Or, as one of my deacons used to say, "It was equally a challenge for Abraham, too—that he at the age of one hundred could produce a child!"

Paul wanted to vindicate God's promise of imputed righteousness given to Abraham. It might be hastily concluded by some that a person justified by faith alone—and apart from works—might not necessarily need to live a holy life. Could not a person abuse this teaching? Yes. But Paul wanted to show that the person who is the recipient of the free gift of God's righteousness would consequently show such gratitude to God by living a blameless life. So God challenged Abraham, *"Walk before me, and be blameless"* (Gen. 17:1).

Abraham demonstrated obedience from that moment. True, he pleaded that Ishmael might still be the promised child (see Gen. 17:18). Abraham was unhappy. He was upset. He was hugely disappointed. But there was never a hint of rebellion. Indeed, *"That is why his faith was 'counted to him as righteousness'"* (Rom. 4:22). That is why. That is the reason. That was the purpose of God imputing righteousness to Abraham. Abraham would demonstrate that the person who has been justified by faith *will live an obedient life.*

The only reason that I think explains God allowing Abraham to wait twenty more years before Sarah could get pregnant is to show that imputed righteousness can be vindicated by imparted righteousness. God could take a sun worshipper and make him a saint. God could save a sinner and turn him or her into godliness that reflects the teaching of the Sermon on the Mount.

When God required circumcision, Abraham did not say, "No. I will not do that." He complied. Likewise, he demonstrated a great and wonderful faith:

> *In hope he believed against hope, that he should become the father of many nations, as he had been told, "So shall your offspring be." He did not weaken in faith when he considered his own body, which was as good as dead (since he was about a hundred years old), or when he considered the barrenness of Sarah's womb. No unbelief made him waver concerning the promise of God, but he grew strong in his faith as he gave glory to God, fully convinced that God was able to do what he had promised. That is why his faith was "counted to him as righteousness"* (Romans 4:18-22).

It is this kind of faith that will enable a believer to come into their inheritance. The letter to the Hebrews elaborates on the teaching of inheritance in Hebrews more than any other Epistle in the New Testament. Hebrews 11—the faith chapter—is not an illustration of how people get saved; it is about persistent faith. The writer of Hebrews wanted to show what people can do who persist in faith! The writer of Hebrews focused on Sarah and Abraham:

> *By faith Sarah herself received power to conceive, even when she was past the age, since she considered him faithful who had promised. Therefore from one man, and him as good as dead, were born descendants as many as the*

stars of heaven and as many as the innumerable grains of
sand by the seashore (Hebrews 11:11-12).

Faith in the blood of Jesus is what saves us. Persistent faith is what
enables us to come into our inheritance. That is what the second half of
Romans 4 is largely about. Indeed, this is not merely for Abraham, says
Paul, but for you and me also:

> *But the words "it was counted to him" were not written*
> *for his sake alone, but for ours also. It will be counted to*
> *us who believe in him who raised from the dead Jesus our*
> *Lord, who was delivered up for our trespasses and raised*
> *for our justification* (Romans 4:23-25).

You and I are called to come into our inheritance. Like it or not,
inheritance assumes a robust faith. Whereas a simple faith in the gospel grants us imputed righteousness, an amazing, persistent faith will
bring you and me into our inheritance.

Is anything too hard for the Lord?
—Genesis 18:14

God will meet you where you are in order to take you where He wants you to go.
—Tony Evans

Chapter Five

ENCOURAGEMENT WHEN WE NEED IT

The purpose of this chapter is to show what lay behind Abraham's strong faith as indicated in the latter part of Romans 4. I hope that this chapter will encourage you to expect the next great move of God on the earth—the move that I call Isaac.

I so hoped to see true revival at Westminster Chapel. It is partly what kept me there. Although we loved England and we loved the British (our closest friends to this day are British), we always thought that one day we would go home. We could never afford to live in London. But I felt I could not leave until my dream was fulfilled. It never was.

MY MINISTRY POST WESTMINSTER

After we had been in London for over twenty-three years, I asked myself one morning, *How long should I stay at Westminster Chapel if revival never comes? When will I give up my dream?* I said to myself, *I will stay twenty-five years.* But a sense of panic set in. I suddenly faced a sobering fact: Nobody knows me in America. We left the United States in 1973. Whatever will I do? I answered myself, *I will become a recluse and bonefish twenty-four hours a day.* We planned to move to the Florida Keys. At that moment, I heard these words: "Your ministry in America will be to Charismatics"—just like that.

I said, "Oh no, please let my ministry be to evangelicals. I have the credentials. I know how evangelicals think. I have what I believe they need."

Sorry. Charismatics.

Sometimes God places us in an area or situation that is not naturally exciting to us. For nearly ten years, I was forced to be in secular work—as a salesman. But it was what I needed. I learned how to handle money. I learned how to be involved with business, people, and situations I would not have chosen. They were preparation for my future. I recall talking to a pastor in the Florida Keys. I said, "Do you realize how blessed you are? You get to live here—beautiful weather, fishing, fun."

He replied, "I would rather live in North Carolina."

I said to a pastor in Fort Lauderdale, "You are so blessed. You get to live in the tropics."

He replied, "I prefer living in Texas."

Paul the apostle wanted his ministry to be to Jews. But he accepted God's will; he would minister to Gentiles (see Gal. 2:9).

But how ever could I have a ministry to Charismatics; how ever could this happen? Three things emerged out of the blue. First, Steve Strang, owner of Charisma House, offered to publish my book *Total Forgiveness*. He also published my book *The Anointing*. His constituency was to Charismatics. Second, I teamed up with Jack Taylor and Charles Carrin to form a trio; we called ourselves "Word, Spirit, Power." I would be the "Word" man, Jack the "Spirit" man, and Charles the "power" man. I did not realize that Jack and Charles had strong charismatic connections. We ended up doing ninety-nine conferences all over America. Third, I had promised to lead a tour to Israel in the summer of 2002. While there, I was invited by Canon Andrew White (the Archbishop of Canterbury's envoy to the Middle East) to meet the late Yasser Arafat, president of the Palestinian Liberation Organization (PLO). I happened to be in California shortly after that. Because I had just been with Arafat, Paul Crouch asked me to be interviewed on "Praise the Lord," sponsored by TBN. All this happened without my effort.

God knows how to encourage us. Doors opened up to me without my raising a little finger. As it turned out, I did little bonefishing. We have since moved to Nashville. No bonefish here.

When God gives a stupendous promise, he has a way of adding a word of encouragement so that we will not give up. When the angel said to the virgin Mary that she would have a child by the Holy Spirit, this word was added: *"For nothing will be impossible with God"* (Luke 1:37). Some promises are more challenging, or extraordinary, than others. Nothing can be more challenging than this: Mary, you will have a baby without there being a father. That is why the angel added, *"For nothing will be impossible with God."* She needed that!

I will come clean. If you ask whether I fully realize that what I am promising in this book is extraordinary, the answer is yes, I think I do. You can say it is extreme. Agreed. It could understandably be seen as going over the top. And I get nervous. Or scared. A word that says that the greatest spiritual awakening since Pentecost is coming is bold. It is putting my 65 years of ministry on the line. It is an overstretch to compare this to Abraham being told that he at almost a hundred and Sarah at the age of ninety would have a baby. But sometimes I feel this way.

According to my father, Dr. R. T. Williams, the man I was named after, gave this advice to young ministers: "Young men, stay away from the subject of prophecy. Let the older men do that. That way they won't be around to see their mistakes!" Yes. Good advice. And I am old. And yet you could say, "You can predict these things, R. T., because you will be gone and won't suffer the pain and embarrassment of seeing how you got it wrong." I accept that. But there is something worse than that; I will also be exposed and found out at the judgment seat of Christ (see 2 Cor. 5:10). I certainly don't want that. For that would be a million times worse than being unvindicated before you. And yet it is my eschatology—not only a prophetic instinct that I felt in my heart nearly fifty years ago—that encourages me to write as I am doing in this book. I do admit that this puts my entire biblical ministry pretty much on the line. I just wish it would be clearly fulfilled while I am alive, assuming that God could trust me with this sort of vindication, as I will go into further below.

As we saw from Romans 4, Abraham wrestled with this. I am *not* saying or even suggesting that God has spoken to me as He did to Abraham. Not at all. I am going entirely on a "hunch" plus my theological belief. God *clearly* spoke directly to Abraham. Paul told us this in Romans 4:18: *"In hope [Abraham] believed against hope."* And yet it is written that *"no unbelief made him waver concerning the promise of God"* (Rom. 4:20). As we saw, Abraham was fully aware that he was nearly ninety-nine, his wife ninety.

My regret as I write this book is that I am so old. I believe what I am writing is true, but I have no *infallible assurance* that Isaac will show up while I am alive. I wish I did. There are levels of assurance. If you put me under a lie detector, I can tell you that I do believe in my heart that the greatest awakening ever—that I call Isaac—is coming. This is because the visions I received back in 1956 made me think I would be alive when it comes. Other visions were fulfilled. Preaching in Ohio that was fulfilled six years later. Preaching in New York that came about sixty years later. Having a ministry that would go around the world that came twenty years later. When I was a door-to-door vacuum cleaner salesman in South Florida, you can be sure I wondered how in the world these visions would be fulfilled. But they were. I was making a living selling vacuum cleaners in 1967; my ministry in London began in 1977.

Abraham believed the initial word about his seed being innumerable as the stars in the heavens. Never forget that it was when he was eighty. His faith counted for righteousness (see Gen. 15:6). When he was told twenty years later—*twenty years later*—that he and Sarah would have a baby, he fell on his face and laughed! Sarah later laughed, too. That hardly sounds like great faith to me. Their laughter, however, did not abort God's plan for them. God merely gave them renewed strength to believe! Yes, at some stage, Abraham *"grew strong in his faith"* so that *"no unbelief made him waver"* concerning the promise that specifically referred to Sarah (Rom. 4:20-21). That initial promise led to Abraham sleeping with Hagar and the birth of Ishmael. *That faith that led to Ishmael, however, is the faith that justified him.* But the promise that Sarah would conceive was incredibly more challenging! And yet he grew strong so that he eventually fully believed that *Sarah* would conceive. And she did!

HOW ABRAHAM RECEIVED ENCOURAGEMENT

What happened to Abraham that enabled him to have faith that Sarah would conceive? It was not when he laughed. It was when three angels visited him. *"Three men"* came near to him. We are told that it was the *"Lord"* (Gen. 18:1). But surely they were angels representing the Most High God. And yet Abraham bowed himself to the earth and said, *"O Lord, if I have found favor in your sight, do not pass by your servant"* (Gen. 18:3). It is written that *"they"*—the three men—spoke to Abraham (Gen. 18:5). That said, a case could be made that they represented the Triune God. It is written that *"two angels"* came later to Sodom (Gen. 19:1). One stayed behind. Two possibly forecasting the Son and the Spirit—members of the Trinity—who would deal directly with humankind; not God the Father who would not look upon sin. In any case, here is what Abraham said to the three angels:

> *"O Lord, if I have found favor in your sight, do not pass by your servant. Let a little water be brought, and wash your feet, and rest yourselves under the tree, while I bring*

a morsel of bread, that you may refresh yourselves, and after that you may pass on—since you have come to your servant." So they said, "Do as you have said" (Genesis 18:3-5).

Abraham then ordered Sarah to prepare a meal for them (see Gen. 18:6).

They said to him, "Where is Sarah your wife?" And he said, "She is in the tent." The Lord said, "I will surely return to you about this time next year, and Sarah your wife shall have a son" (Genesis 18:9-10).

My point here is, this is the first confirmation of what God said to Abraham earlier about Sarah having a baby—when Abraham laughed. But this angelic visitation must surely have made Abraham see that this indeed is a no-joke thing. Not only that, Sarah overheard the conversation between the angels and Abraham. Apparently, it was the first time she knew anything about her going to have a baby at the age of ninety. Abraham had not told her what the Lord told him (see Gen. 17:15ff). So when she heard the conversation between Abraham and these three angels—that she would have a son—Sarah laughed. She said to herself, *"After I am worn out, and my lord [Abraham] is old, shall I have pleasure?"* (Gen. 18:12). Then *"the Lord said to Abraham, 'Why did Sarah laugh and say, "Shall I indeed bear a child, now that I am old?"'... But Sarah denied it... for she was afraid. [Abraham] said, 'No, but you did laugh'"* (Gen. 18:13-15).

The above proved to Abraham and Sarah that she *really and truly* would have a baby! The angelic visit was a confirmation of the word given earlier to Abraham. The angels—the Lord—said, *"Is anything too hard for the Lord?"* (Gen. 18:14). This is the equivalent of the angel saying to the virgin Mary, *"Nothing shall be impossible with God"* (Luke 1:37).

Encouragement was what Abraham needed in order to believe indeed what God had said to him at the time he learned that Ishmael was not the promised son. Maybe Abraham believed it then; maybe he didn't. But with the angelical visitation—the word confirming the earlier promise—Abraham now took this very seriously. It was the angelic visitation that enabled him to grow strong in his faith.

There is more. Abraham's strong faith had led him to be truly righteous—a godly man. As we have seen, Genesis 15:6 refers to an imputed righteousness. But after the covenant of circumcision, Abraham was commanded to be *"blameless"* (Gen. 17:1). This meant an *imparted* righteousness. Abraham had now become truly godly. It was a strong faith that *came after* Abraham accepted God's word that Ishmael was not the promised child. It was a different Abraham.

I think the angelic encouragement that Abraham received was *almost* like having God swear an oath to him. But it was not that. That would not come until after Isaac was born. That said, something gave Abraham a greater measure of faith than he had had before. *The imputed righteousness that came in Genesis 15:6 had become an imparted righteousness after the angelic visitation.* This increased faith is what Paul picked up on in the second part of Romans 4.

God gave Abraham encouragement when he needed it. You may have heard the expression "To hell and back." Here is a better phrase: "To Heaven and back." It is when you experience the immediate and direct witness of the Spirit. The phrase "immediate and direct" came to me from Dr. Martyn Lloyd-Jones. It is the immediate and direct witness of the Spirit that will persuade a man or woman of the Bible being the Word of God. Likewise, it is the immediate and direct witness of the Spirit that will give us encouragement when we need it!

One of the reasons for this chapter is that you, the reader, might be encouraged that Isaac is coming. As for my own encouragement that I will see the next great awakening, I have not had an angelic visitation. God has not sworn an oath to me that I will be alive when the next great move of God on the earth emerges. My only hope that I will see the coming move of God while I am alive is that I saw myself in these visions.

One more thing. My fear that I won't see the coming move of God while I am still alive is possibly that I would swell up with pride and take myself too seriously. I share a story that makes me think this.

John Paul Jackson told me that, when he "came to earth" (as it were) after being taken to Heaven in a lengthy vision, he was depressed for several days. He lay on the floor and said, "God, I am angry with You. You showed me Your power. What You can do. I could stand in front of a Dallas hospital and pray and see every patient instantly healed. Why won't You do this?" John Paul then said that the Lord replied, "John Paul, if I gave you that much power, I would have to judge you. You could not cope with the fame this would give you."

I tell the above story because I sometimes wonder if I will not be allowed to see the coming of Isaac for the similar reasoning. I have prayed that God would equip me and enable me to cope with sufficient humility if my word about Isaac were fulfilled while I am alive. I cannot be sure what I would be like. This, then, is my fear.

Is there anything you and I can do to hasten the coming of Isaac? I doubt it. It is my opinion that it will come suddenly without our help and that nobody can stop it when it begins.

ENCOURAGEMENT FROM SMITH WIGGLESWORTH

Smith Wigglesworth said that, with a new move of the Spirit, those in it will say, "This is *the* great revival" (or words like that). This is the way many have regarded the charismatic movement. This is not surprising. Wigglesworth said also that these moves of the Spirit are steps toward it. Jonathan Edwards thought that what people were experiencing in his day, now called the Great Awakening (c. 1730–1740), was "it"— that is, the coming of the glory of the Lord as the waters cover the sea. Edwards is to be forgiven for thinking this!

Will the next great move of God be exactly like the first Pentecost? I don't know. But it will be just as convincing, just as real, and just as evangelistic. Mockers will bend the knee to a sovereign God. *"What shall we do?"* will be asked by surprised people, as they asked on the Day of Pentecost (Acts 2:37). The answer will be the same: Repent and receive the gospel of Jesus Christ. The death and resurrection of Jesus Christ from the dead will be preached with power and without compromise. The awareness of the true God—who He is and what He has done in His Son—will be revived and real. For those who are saved, it will be like being "to Heaven and back"—only to wait for the glorious second coming of Jesus.

Not all will be saved. But all will behold the return of the fear of God. People will believe that Jesus is coming again. And that He is coming soon.

Are you so foolish? Having begun by the Spirit,
are you now being perfected by the flesh?
—Galatians 3:3

The church is always to be under the Word; she must
be; we must keep her there. You must not assume that
because the church started correctly, she will continue so.
She did not do so in New Testament times; she has not
done so since. Without being constantly reformed by the
Word, the church becomes very different.
—Martyn Lloyd-Jones (1899–1981)

The worst thing that can happen to a man
is to succeed before he is ready.
—Martyn Lloyd-Jones

Chapter Six

THE GOOD, THE BAD, THE UGLY

Some readers will see that I have made good use of this chapter title. The famous movie title *The Good, the Bad and the Ugly* with Clint Eastwood cannot be improved on when it comes to some themes. I wrote the book *Fear: The Good* [fear of God], *the Bad* [fear of man], *and the Ugly* [satanic fear]. In my book *Prophetic Integrity*, I wrote about the prophetic movement in terms of the good, the bad, and the ugly. I do so now with regard to the Pentecostal-charismatic movement.

THE GOOD

This book is about the charismatic movement. One of the knotty problems I have had to deal with is how the charismatic movement has become partly an extension of the Pentecostal movement but also how it sprang from historic denominations and in a sense is disconnected from the historic Pentecostal movement. It is not always a clear-cut issue. As noted previously, the emergence of the charismatic movement, also once called the glossolalia movement, seems to have appeared around 1960. The fact that these emerged independently of each other—in Seattle, South Africa, and England—suggests that the charismatic movement was a genuine work of God. I would contend that the charismatic movement began in the Spirit. The common denominator would almost certainly be speaking in tongues.

The Emphasis on the Holy Spirit

The single, most obvious, and truly glorious aspect of the charismatic movement is calling attention to the person and work of the Third Person of the Godhead—the Holy Spirit. The word *charismata* means "grace-gifts." Jesus introduced His disciples to "another" *parakletos*—a word that means "one who comes alongside." Jesus had come alongside His disciples for some three years. The disciples were not thrilled when they heard Jesus talk about "another" Comforter, Advocate, or Helper. They wanted Jesus Himself to stay with them. But no. He would go away in order for another Helper to come.

The Helper came on the Day of Pentecost. The book of Acts is a demonstration of the Word and the Spirit. Tertullian (c. 155–c. 220) coined the Latin words *trinitas* and *persona*. Hence, to this day we speak of the "three persons of the Trinity." Tertullian is also often referred to as the first Charismatic following the days of the apostles. He got involved in the controversial Montanist Movement that had a huge emphasis on the Spirit. In the fourth century, Saint Augustine gave us the doctrine of original sin and predestination. Athanasius emphasized Jesus as the God-man. The Reformers, beginning with

Martin Luther, revived Paul's teaching of justification by faith. I am skipping over many great men and also many moments of true revival. These movements had sound doctrines regarding the Holy Spirit. But these doctrines were largely soteriological doctrines of the Spirit—meaning the indirect and mediate work of the Spirit, not direct and immediate. The idea of *experiencing* the Spirit was pretty much unknown. English Puritans such as John Cotton (1585–1652) and Thomas Goodwin (1600–1680) made some references to this, but overall, the idea of experiencing the Spirit was unknown.

With the falling of the Spirit on Azusa Street in 1906, the modern Pentecostal movement was born. Then came the charismatic movement around 1960. These movements had in common the gifts of the Spirit and the emphasis was largely on speaking in tongues. I am passing over other movements, the Latter Rain movement, for example.

My point is this. The Church generally is indebted to Charismatics and Pentecostals for the emphasis of *experiencing* the immediate and direct witness of the Holy Spirit.

This is good. Very, very good.

The healing movement—with people like Oral Roberts, William Branham (1909–1965), Paul Cain, and others—became prominent in the 1950s, happening often in large tent meetings. I got to know Paul Cain very well and visited Oral Roberts three times in his California home. There is no doubt in my mind that there were miraculous healings in the ministries of these men.

Paul Cain, Oral Roberts, and John Paul Jackson came out of the Pentecostal movement. But they became popular with Charismatics, and people tend to forget about or not know about their Pentecostal backgrounds. Paul Cain was a Baptist before he went into the Assemblies of God. He was accepted by many Anglicans in Britain. Oral Roberts became a Methodist. John Paul was a part of the Assemblies of God and later became a part of the Vineyard Movement with John Wimber.

There is no doubt in my mind that these men had a genuine touch of God on them; they had powerful anointings.

Paul Cain told me this story, this being one of the most memorable healings in his ministry. He said that the Lord showed him that there would be a couple present in that evening's tent meeting who would "kidnap" their three-year-old crippled child from the hospital. The child had polio and disproportionately small legs. The Lord told him, Paul said, that it would be a creative miracle. He said that he could think of nothing else all day and could hardly wait for the evening service to come. Soon after the service began, he spotted the couple—way in the back of the tent—with the child hidden in a blanket and on their laps. Paul called them out. They were afraid to raise their hands or stand because their child had been secretly taken from the hospital. They were hoping the child might be healed without having to do anything. But Paul assured them it would be okay if they stood and brought the child forward. I will tell you, reader, as I type this I come to tears, recalling how Paul related the story. Right after the couple stepped into the aisle, the child slipped through the blanket and went onto the floor before everyone's eyes. The little legs were stretched to normal size, and the child *walked* with his parents to the front! He said the crowd went wild with excitement.

Paul shared several stories that clearly showed the supernatural. He showed me photographs that someone gave him. These showed miracles from the early 1950s. Healed people, for example, carried their own wheelchairs home. He said there were many people healed who had been afflicted with polio. Goiters being healed was common. But, said Paul, the anointing lifted. There had been evenings in which *everyone* who wanted healing was healed. But for some reason—around 1954—people who came for prayer were stopped from being healed. He added that other "faith healers [as they were called] would not admit that the anointing lifted but kept pretending that people were still being healed." There were no doubt some exceptions. But Paul chose to leave the public ministry and became a recluse for many years, living with his mother. However, for some reason, although his healing gift seemed to diminish, his prophetic gift remained. After being discovered by John Wimber for his amazing prophetic gift, he traveled with Wimber to places such as Australia and England. I met Paul in 1990. He later became a member of Westminster Chapel. I know for a fact that his prophetic gift was genuine. Many of his stories sounded like those right out of the days of Elisha. I only wish I had recorded these. I can't remember most of them in detail.

Fast-forward to 2002. Steve Strang took me to meet Oral Roberts. Without my asking him, Oral Roberts wrote a lengthy foreword to my book *Total Forgiveness*. And later, at my request, he wrote a foreword to my book *Totally Forgiving Ourselves*. While with him on one of the three visits I would have with him, he shared a "revelation" he said he got from the Lord about the coming move of God. He wept as he said that, whereas Israel missed their Messiah, "This time they will get in on it" (or words to that effect). What he described absolutely paralleled what this book is about. Great revival was coming.

He took me into the hallway of his home and said two things: (1) that this was where he was when this revelation came to him, then added, (2) that it was his "old anointing." This to me was and is a very, very telling phrase. Call it a throw-away statement; it was an implicit admission of the anointing that once characterized his ministry. I don't want to put words in his mouth, but it told me that he had not experienced this for a good while. As I said above, he left the Pentecostal Holiness denomination and became a Methodist. But he later returned to his old denomination. I do believe he was a sincere man of God. I fear, however, that he got off the rails in some ways. I knew he would welcome the opportunity to write the foreword to my book *Totally Forgiving Ourselves*. I will add that, when I visited him for the third time, I took Louise with me. He prayed for us and gently laid his hand on Louise, and she felt such power that she could hardly stand. I treasure, most of all, a word he gave me: "Do nothing until you feel the anointing." His wife, Evelyn gave me one of his ties!

In January 1991, John Wimber invited Louise and me to California to attend his conference and to spend time with Paul Cain. I am not sure it was justified, as some did, to refer to John Wimber or his Vineyard movement as the "Third Way," but I was impressed with Wimber. So too was J. I. Packer. Dr. Packer, who almost certainly was the most respected Reformed theologian in the world, was no cessationist and implicitly endorsed the Toronto Blessing. It was Wimber who took Paul Cain, Bob Jones, and John Paul Jackson to England. This is how I met all these men. In 1994, the aforementioned Toronto Blessing broke out. Because of some reports of strange manifestations in Toronto, Wimber put Pastor John Arnott and the Toronto Vineyard Fellowship out of the movement. But on his deathbed, he told John Paul Jackson that disenfranchising the Toronto Vineyard was the greatest mistake of his life.

If I may add a footnote, I was invited by John Arnott to speak for him on the second anniversary of the Toronto Blessing in January 1996. Something strange happened to me that evening—unprecedented—and has not happened since. When I began to speak during that unforgettable evening, suddenly I could hardly talk. It was so embarrassing. I could not make a single intelligible sentence. This lasted several minutes. You can order the video (their best-selling video, I am told). All at once Hebrews 13:13 came to mind. I quickly turned to see what it said: *"Let us go unto him outside the camp, bearing his reproach."* At last, I could speak. My tongue was loosed! I soared for several minutes. Hundreds came forward after I spoke that evening. But here is why I add this footnote: It was the first service in the Toronto Church with the new name: Toronto Airport Fellowship. The name "Vineyard" was then removed. They were officially "outside the camp."

The Best Hymns of Our Generation

Ninety percent of the hymns that have been popular in the past fifty years have been written by charismatic composers and musicians. Many of these hymns or songs are sung in nearly *all* denominations. I am privileged to know some of these composers and singers—men like Graham Kendrick ("Shine Jesus Shine"), Chris Bowater ("Here I am, wholly available"), and Matt Redman ("Ten Thousand Reasons," better known as "Bless the Lord O My Soul"). In my opinion, one of the greatest divine affirmations of the charismatic movement has been the songs that have sprung from it. I could list hundreds more. I am frequently amused to be in a non-charismatic church when they sing some of these hymns. "In Christ Alone" by Keith Getty and Stuart Townend was voted in the past two years to be the favorite hymn in Britain, surpassing "Amazing Grace" and "How Great Thou Art."

The Spreading of the Gospel in the Third World

The teaching of cessationism is almost nonexistent in the Third World. This is because the kind of Christianity that has permeated Third World countries has been preached by those who believe in and practice the gifts of the Spirit as seen in 1 Corinthians 12. Whether we speak of Latin America, South America, or Africa, the kind of Christianity that has largely swept such continents is charismatic. The majority of Christian converts speak in tongues. It has been observed that one of the reasons Christians in these countries persist in much higher numbers than in the United States is because pastors often quickly cast demons out of new converts. This sort of thing is rarely done in the United States. Christianity in China has advanced so amazingly in recent years that, in the next few years, China will be the largest Christian nation in the world. The Christians in China are largely charismatic.

Christian Television

As I type these lines, I am flying back from Springfield, Missouri. Today, I was the guest on Jim Bakker's show. Jim Bakker is a pioneer of

Christian television. He founded the PTL network. Other Christian networks followed, such as TBN and Daystar. In 1989, Jim Bakker was unlawfully sentenced to 45 years in prison. During that time, Tammy Faye divorced him. While in prison, someone sent him my book *God Meant It for Good*. Jim claims it changed his life. He said it is "the greatest book ever written outside the Bible."

After Jim was released from prison in 1994, he came to see me in Florida during one of our summer holidays when I was at Westminster Chapel. I took him bonefishing every day for nearly a week. I married Jim and Lori a couple years later in California. At their wedding, I met the lawyer who was responsible for getting Jim out of prison. He told me all the details. Although Jim said, "God put me in prison," the lawyer said Jim never got a fair trial and never did what he was accused of doing. I wrote a handwritten note to the famous non-charismatic Baptist pastor who was responsible for Jim's false charge. I told him that he would be seriously judged by God if he did not publicly apologize for what he did to Jim Bakker.

THE BAD

I think the Christian TV networks started well. But eventually the "health and wealth, name it and claim it, believe it and receive it" kind of prosperity teaching not only got in but became prominent. What started as good began to drift toward the bad. Mind you, my friend Jim Bakker, while he did nothing illegal, got himself into financial bondage. He told me he had to raise two million dollars every three days. He also said that he came to grips with the sinfulness of prosperity teaching when in prison. His own careful study of the Bible led him to realize its lack of biblical warrant but also his own personal error. In any case, the whole scenario of Jim and Tammy Faye Bakker did not help the reputation of the Christian faith.

So we now must approach the bad. This is *my* opinion. I do not speak for my publisher or the kind people who have endorsed this book. I am thinking of those also in the healing movement who would not admit that the anointing lifted—but continued in ministry. We thank God for those who have had a healing ministry. I wish I had one.

The issue is integrity—whether we will admit it when people are not healed.

It is easy to run ahead of God. Joseph and Mary did this, going a day's journey without the child Jesus and assuming Him to be in their company (see Luke 2:44).

I have not dealt with some of the better-known men and women— some I have met, some I haven't. I won't mention their names partly because I don't have reliable information. For example, I don't know enough about Jack Coe (1918–1956) or A. A. Allen (1911–1970) or Kathryn Kuhlman (1907–1976). But this much I know. When the healing anointing lifted from some of these, their emphasis often shifted to prosperity teaching. I am not their judge, but I suspect it might have something to do with ways to keep their ministries afloat. They appealed to people to give financially. It is often called "seed faith." The idea is, you sow a seed in one's ministry and you will be blessed. Sadly, this often turned to appealing to people's sense of greed. Worse than that, it was often poor people who supported them. It reminds one of those who depend on the lottery. It is sad, and it is bad. I speak as a Bible teacher. If I truly understand the God of the Bible, I fear He would not be happy with these kinds of ministries. I don't mean to be unfair, but I am fearful that the concept of a God of glory is alien to some of these people. I certainly agree that there is truth to the principle of giving and being blessed. This, however, has a lot to do with tithing (see Mal. 3:8-10). But TV ministries often would not want to talk much about "storehouse tithing," which refers to giving to one's local church.

In my book *Prophetic Integrity,* I spoke about my relationship with some of the prophets. I'm sorry, but some of them had in common that they did not read their Bibles. This was a shocking discovery for me. First, I could not help but discern that they were not theologically minded, but second, they did not *know* their Bibles because they did not *read* their Bibles. I persuaded some of them to adopt a Bible reading plan. Dr. Lloyd-Jones introduced the Robert Murray M'Cheyne (1813–1843) Bible Reading Plan to me in 1977. This takes one through the Bible in a year, the New Testament and Psalms twice a year. I succeeded in getting two of them to use this. One of them kept it up for several months. Another continued indefinitely and was keen to tell me how much he was enjoying it.

These are not bad men! But it is bad when people are prominent in ministry and don't know their Bibles! These are not bad men, but they are sad men.

When the anointing lifts, we may discover what we are like as persons. It might be compared to a preacher who wears a robe when he ministers or wears a clerical collar. The issue is, what is the man himself like? That then is the question we might put what is a person like without this anointing of healing?

We know what Elijah was like after his victory over the false prophets of Baal. He proved to be a coward—scared to death of Jezebel (see 1 Kings 19:3).

When we stand before the Lord Jesus Christ on the Final Day, we will give an account for what we have done *"in the body, whether good or evil"* (2 Cor. 5:10). We will not be rewarded for our successes; that has happened on earth. I will not be rewarded for being a preacher or an author. I am recognized for that now. I will be judged by what kind of husband I was, what kind of father, and what kind of a servant of Jesus. It will come out then whether I have sought the honor that comes from the only God, whether I have lived a life of total forgiveness, whether I have been faithful in gratitude by my giving, or whether I demonstrated a life of obedience to Holy Scripture and the voice of the Holy Spirit (see John 5:44; Eph. 4:32).

What will it matter what people think of you or me after we die? Why would good people work overtime to make sure they are remembered well here on earth after they die? What matters is what will come out at the judgment seat of Christ. *That is all that matters.*

Two men in the Bible wanted to ensure they would be sufficiently honored. They chose a statue to honor themselves: King Saul and Absalom the son of David (see 1 Sam. 15:12; 2 Sam. 18:18). Both were utter failures on earth but hoped somehow they would be remembered after they were gone. They got their wish! But their monuments only remind one of their sad endings.

There are those whose reward is only *"in this life"* (Ps. 17:14). A prominent, non-charismatic Baptist pastor hired the best sculptor in America to make a bronze statue of himself and was even present for the unveiling! I always admired this man, and I am not his judge. But frankly, I would not want to be in his shoes at the judgment seat of Christ for anything in this world.

Whether Pentecostal, charismatic, non-charismatic, Calvinist, or Arminian, what we have been as Christian men and women is what matters in eternity. As for the television evangelists, the faith healers, and the prophets, I am sure they all started out to follow the Lord. I don't think a single one of these prominent people were phonies. Most of them were probably converted when young. They wanted to follow the Lord, answer His call on their lives, and bring honor and glory to Him. They started well.

King Saul

First Samuel 16:1 shows three categories of people—yesterday's man, today's man, and tomorrow's man:

> *The Lord said to Samuel, "How long will you grieve over Saul, since I have rejected him from being king over Israel? Fill your horn with oil, and go. I will send you to Jesse the Bethlehemite, for I have provided for myself a king among his sons."*

Saul was yesterday's man even though he remained king of Israel for *another twenty years*. What makes one yesterday's man (or woman) is the lifting of the anointing. It is when one becomes stone deaf to the Holy Spirit—as in Hebrews 6:4-6. King Saul no longer heard from God. Among his last words were these: *"God has turned away from me and answers me no more, either by prophets or by dreams"* (1 Sam. 28:15).

Saul was not a bad man. He was a sad man. But his example is bad. He would not listen to Samuel.

A good beginning does not guarantee a good ending. King Saul started well. He was given *"another heart"* (1 Sam. 10:9). He was given a prophetic gift that was so noticeable the people said, *"Is Saul also among the prophets?"* (1 Sam. 10:12). He had a brilliant beginning as the first king of Israel.

> *The Spirit of God rushed upon Saul.... He took a yoke of oxen and cut them in pieces and sent them throughout all the territory of Israel by the hand of the messengers, saying, "Whoever does not come out after Saul and Samuel, so shall it be done to his oxen!" Then the dread of the Lord fell upon the people, and they came out as one man* (1 Samuel 11:6-7).

What a wonderful start! Who would have dreamed that in a short period of time King Saul would become yesterday's man (see 1 Sam. 16:1)? Yesterday's man? Yes. Not only that, he remained king for twenty years. Only the prophet Samuel realized that the anointing had been lifted from King Saul.

The Bethlehemite was young David. Samuel came to the house of Jesse and poured oil on David, anointing him, *"and the Spirit of the*

Lord rushed upon David from that day forward" (1 Sam. 16:13). David had the undoubted anointing of the Spirit of God but did not become king for another twenty years.

I fear there are those in the pulpit today who are yesterday's men. This refers not to retirement, to age, or to being made redundant. "Yesterday's man" refers to the absence of the anointing. You can be old and be tomorrow's man. Moses was not mightily used of God until he was eighty. You can be young and be yesterday's man. King Saul was only forty when the anointing was lifted from him.

Consider the difference between Saul and David. Saul was king; David was a nobody. Saul had the power and authority; David had neither. Saul had the following; David had no following. Saul had the platform; David had no platform.

Therefore, a man can be in prominence. He may be powerful and popular. He has the mailing list and a great following. But in God's sight, he is yesterday's man.

I see Samuel as a "type" of today's man. He was required to go outside his comfort zone: God said, *"I will send you to Jesse the Bethlehemite"* (1 Sam. 16:1). Samuel replied, *"If Saul hears it, he will kill me"* (1 Sam. 16:2). I learn from the latter verse that the way to keep from becoming yesterday's man is to be willing *always* to go outside your comfort zone. Samuel was old. A legend. But God was not finished with him yet.

I now write a word of encouragement to anyone who wants to embrace this: As long as you remain willing to go outside your comfort zone, God is not finished with you.

But if you refuse to go outside your comfort zone, God will look for those who are willing to do this.

The most memorable comment Dr. Lloyd-Jones ever made to me was this: "The worst thing that can happen to a man is for him to succeed before he is ready."

That is what happened to Saul.

THE UGLY

Dear reader, I am fully aware that the Lord Jesus said, *"Judge not, that you be not judged"* (Matt. 7:1). I am conscious that Paul said to judge nothing before the time but wait until God reveals His opinion of all of us (see 1 Cor. 4:5). This includes judging the motives of individuals. It largely refers to when you have a personal enemy—that is, when someone has hurt you, vilified you, or spoken against you. This is why Jesus said earlier in the Sermon on the Mount that you should bless and pray for your enemy. Praying for God to bless your enemy—praying this from the heart—is the hardest thing in the world to do. At first. But it eventually becomes as if it were a selfish thing! The blessing from it is so wonderful. Indeed, it's beyond my ability to describe.

In my case—but I predict equally in your case—the worst thing that ever happened to me turned out to be the best thing that ever happened to me. It was during my days at Westminster Chapel—during the darkest hour Louise and I had ever gone through. It was when Josif Ton (pronounced Tson) of Romania said to me, "R. T., you must *totally* forgive them; until you *totally* forgive them, you will be in chains. Release them, and you will be released." Those words changed my life. It led to my praying for those who had brought on my darkest hour. I cannot exaggerate the blessing that has come to us since. If you haven't done this, I urge you—do it.

That said, the charismatic movement is not my enemy. My debt to Charismatics is incalculable. As Westminster Chapel gave me my ministry to the United Kingdom, the charismatic movement gave me a ministry to the world. I am indebted to Steve Strang, TBN, Daystar, the late Jack Taylor, Charles Carrin, and others. There is nothing personal in what I have to say when I point out the "ugly" in the charismatic movement.

I am also aware that Paul said, *"The spiritual person judges all things"* (1 Cor. 2:15). Furthermore, it was not personal when John felt it necessary to warn people about Diotrephes (see 3 John 1:9–11). I repeat, I am not an apostle, and I am not a prophet. I feel it is necessary to keep saying that I am only a Bible teacher. If it was the Lord—this is a big "if"—that was behind the unforgettable thought I had in Oxford in 1973, I am only following through with my instinct. Time and events will decide whether I have gotten it right.

I am not saying the unhappy things that have often characterized the charismatic movement are necessarily a sign of God's judgment on it. But I believe that the prophetic element within it is. As God sent a lying spirit to Israel in the days of Elisha, I believe that is truly what has happened in recent years (see 1 Kings 22). The charismatic movement is characterized by men and women saved by grace, those who like you and me are imperfect. In other words, I do not say at all that the things I mention in this section are the reason that the charismatic movement is Ishmael. It is my view that the original Ishmael, firstborn son of Abraham, was a non-starter from the beginning—that God *always* had Isaac in mind. So, too, is it God's purpose and plan to bless the Church of Jesus Christ with much, much more than our generation has seen—or even imagined. These things said, we must always remember that God's ways are higher than our ways, His thoughts vastly different from our thoughts. There always will be things God doesn't want us completely to figure out.

I mention four things that—to my way of thinking—are ugly.

1. A Prophetic Word Having Priority over Scripture

There is a perspective among some people in influence that a "word of knowledge" or a prophetic word supersedes Holy Scripture. One very high-profile charismatic leader told me that he believed his word of knowledge was to be obeyed rather than Scripture. There is one person I know who has a very high profile but who apparently does not have time to read his Bible. So, because he has access to a man who alleges to have accurate word of knowledge, he contacts him often to ask, "What would the Lord have me say or do today?" In other words, he seeks the prophetic word vis-à-vis turning to the Holy Scripture.

I call this ugly. A person like this is not seeking a close relationship with God but is only "using" God for his own benefit. Sadly, many people today do not know their Bibles because they do not read their Bibles.

The highest respect we can pay to the Holy Spirit is to embrace and extol His greatest product—the Bible. Why is this? It is because the Spirit of God wrote it. In Paul's last letter before he died, he said,

All Scripture is breathed out by God and profitable for teaching, for reproof, for correction, and for training in righteousness, that the man of God may be complete, equipped for every good work (2 Timothy 3:16–17).

Peter wrote,

For no prophecy was ever produced by the will of man, but men spoke from God as they were carried along by the Holy Spirit (2 Peter 1:21).

I would note two things. First, Scripture is breathed out by the Holy Spirit. The Spirit of God is the Author of Scripture. The Bible is the Holy Spirit's greatest product. Second, one of the purposes of Scripture is that we might *"be complete."* To the degree we neglect Holy Scripture we are *incomplete.* No matter how many words of knowledge or prophetic words we may receive, we are *incomplete* without the knowledge the Bible can give us. I'm sorry, but so many people today—whether lay people or those in leadership—whether pastors, prophets, or evangelists—are often theologically shallow and do not know their Bibles. I wish I were wrong.

I was asked by someone two years ago, "What would you like to accomplish before you die?" I answered, "To get people to take the Bible seriously." I could happily die and go to Heaven if I thought I made a difference in this area. I believe that Protestantism generally is in virtually the same state that the Church was in hundreds of years ago when God raised up John Wycliffe (c. 1328–1384), who translated the Latin Bible into English, and William Tyndale (c. 1494–1536), who translated the Bible into English from the Greek. Both got into serious trouble with the church authorities for insisting that common people—not just the priests—read the Bible. Wycliffe once told a priest, "If God spares my life, I will cause a boy that drives a plough to know more of the Scriptures than you do." Wycliffe barely escaped being burned at the stake. Tyndale, in fact, died as a martyr. His crime: to get the ordinary person to read the Bible. The difference between then and now is that then people didn't have Bibles; nowadays people have Bibles but barely believe them.

Virtually 100 percent of the prophetic people who spoke regarding the 2020 election prophesied that Donald Trump would be reelected for a second term in 2020. They said that *God* told them; "thus says the Lord" was behind their predictions. (Only Ron Cantor, as I say in *Prophetic Integrity*, said that Joe Biden would win.) I personally think that this huge miss is a clear sign of God's judgment. Yes, I am convinced that the prophetic movement is a confirmation that the charismatic movement is Ishmael.

2. Pompous Overclaiming

For example, this mentality says, "If the apostle Paul had my faith, he would not have had his thorn in the flesh." A well-known prosperity preacher made this claim. This is, in my opinion, bordering on the most presumptuous and arrogant if not blasphemous statement I have heard in my lifetime. I double-checked to see if I heard correctly. I asked one of his followers. Their reply: "Oh yes, that is what we are taught."

I cannot imagine the apostle Paul bragging on himself like that—boasting that his faith would prevent a thorn in the flesh! Paul, showing transparent humility, said that God sent this because of Paul's prone-ness to being conceited! He openly admitted that he was prone to be conceited. Aren't we all? Saying *"I am the very least of all the saints"* was typical of Paul (Eph. 3:8). The background of his own thorn in the flesh was his weakness, which he admitted to—being conceited. Indeed, he made it clear that he would boast not of his strength—which this preacher did—but of his weakness (see 2 Cor. 11:30). He regarded himself as the chief of sinners (see 1 Tim. 1:15)! But more than that is his own word that he was *"an example to those who were to believe"* in Jesus (1 Tim. 1:16). But if we reject the idea that Paul was an example, we likewise reject Scripture!

It is my own observation that many of us Charismatics either have no sense of sin or feel no need to think along those lines. John said that, if we say we have no sin, we *"deceive ourselves, and the truth is not in us"* (1 John 1:8). One of the great hymns of the Church begins with the line "Come Thou Fount of Every Blessing." One of the verses in this hymn says this:

> Oh, to grace how great a debtor
> Daily I'm constrained to be;
> Let Thy goodness like a fetter
> Bind my wandering heart to Thee.
> Prone to wander, Lord, I feel it,
> Prone to leave the God I love;
> Here's my heart, oh take and seal it;
> Seal it for Thy courts above.

—Robert Robinson (1735–1790)

This is normal Christian experience. But it is alien to many in the holiness movement and to many Charismatics. One denomination included this hymn in their standard hymnal but changed the words from "Bind my wandering heart to Thee" to "Bind my yielded heart to Thee," and the words "Prone to wander, Lord, I feel it" to "Let me know Thee in Thy fullness."

It is a curious fact that, when reading the biographies of the great saints in history, the greatest saints always saw themselves as the greatest sinners. But some prosperity teachers imply we can out-do Paul and the great saints in history. Reader, we will never be sinless until we are in Heaven! I was recently interviewed on a charismatic TV show regarding my book *You Might Be a Pharisee If...* I mentioned to the interviewer that the Pharisees had no sense of sin. The man clearly did not know how to discuss this. With ten minutes left for the show to continue, he abruptly said, "Thank you, Dr. Kendall, for being with us today" and closed the program! Talking about having a sense of sin was out of his depth.

3. Gifting More Important than Character

Strange as it may seem, we now see the polar opposite to the previous discussion. There are those leaders who are claiming that, if a person has a spectacular prophetic gift—or healing gift—his or her personal life is not of great importance. There are those who are so keen to see genuine miracles that they will turn a blind eye when it comes to a person's corrupt character.

One of the things that attracted me to the late John Paul Jackson was his adamant stance on a person's personal godly character. He shared with me some of the harsh criticisms from high-profile leaders who felt that the need of the hour was miracles and more miracles—so much so that one's sexual conduct could be overlooked.

Billy Graham said before he died that "it seems that the devil gets seventy-five percent of God's best leaders through sexual temptation." Billy's closest friend was T. W. Wilson, whom I got to know very well. Billy never traveled alone and made sure that someone was always with him. T. W. told me that when Billy was away from home, he always slept in the same hotel room with Billy to make sure nobody could ever accuse Billy of sexual immorality. But some charismatic leaders are not so careful. This is one of the reasons that some of the best-known charismatic preachers have made front page news by their immorality.

Here is the strangest thing yet. I don't understand it. But I know for a fact that some of those with the greatest healing or prophetic gifts can indulge in sexual misconduct and not have the slightest negative effect on the effectiveness of their gift. Sadly, there are those who feel that God obviously overlooks moral flaws or He would not use their gifts as He apparently has done.

On his way to murder young David, King Saul prophesied. The thing that mystifies me is that *the Spirit of God* came on Saul and he prophesied. Indeed, the people were so taken by Saul's prophesying that they said, *"Is Saul also among the prophets?"* (1 Sam. 19:23-24). I have wondered what it was that Saul said. I believe we will get to see a video replay of things like this that some find fascinating.

How would the apostle Paul feel about gifting being more important than character? He would be utterly appalled. Paul stressed godliness and holy living as much as he did sovereign grace and faith. Listen to his words to Timothy:

> *Do not neglect the gift you have, which was given you by prophecy when the council of elders laid their hands on you. Practice these things, immerse yourself in them, so that all may see your progress. Keep a close watch on yourself and on the teaching. Persist in this, for by so doing you will save both yourself and your hearers* (1 Timothy 4:14-16).

> *If anyone teaches a different doctrine and does not agree with the sound words of our Lord Jesus Christ and the teaching that accords with godliness, he is puffed up with conceit and understands nothing* (1 Timothy 6:3-4).

> *If anyone cleanses himself from what is dishonorable, he will be a vessel for honorable use, set apart as holy, useful to the master of the house, ready for every good work* (2 Timothy 2:21).

It ought to be a principle beyond controversy or need for discussion that character is more important than one's gift. It will be one's character, not his or her gifting, that will be under scrutiny at the judgment seat of Christ (see 2 Cor. 5:10).

4. The Entry of Open Theism

It is hard to say which of the four "ugly" examples in this section is the ugliest. But I would vote for open theism as being the worst thing ever to emerge among Charismatics. This is a teaching barely recognized by most but unconsciously embraced by many Charismatics and evangelicals. A teacher at Fuller Theological Seminary, but widely appreciated as a leader in the charismatic movement, managed to get this deadly teaching into the thinking of many Charismatics several years ago. When I was at my old seminary, it was merely called "process theology" and was within a hair's breadth of sheer atheism. It is essentially pantheism. Pantheism is the belief that all is God—that is, nature: trees, grass, animals, people. But this is given an evangelical dress by some who find it attractive.

One difference between the proponents of process theology and the open theism embraced today is that process theology denied all the historic truths: virgin birth, bodily resurrection, need for people to be saved, the second coming, and the final judgment. Today, both charismatic and evangelical leaders attempt to hold on to these truths but deny that God knows the future. Many open theists would likely be either universalists or annihilationists. I doubt if an open theist can be found who believes in conscious eternal punishment.

The way many Charismatics apply open theism to the teaching of prayer—even though they don't know the term—is to believe that God answers prayer but *only with our help*. I give this teaching a lot of attention in my book *Prophetic Integrity*. In a word, open theism holds that God does not know the future. He only knows possibilities. He needs us. He cannot do anything without us. Open theism reduces God to a contingency planner; He knows every possibility but does not know which path you and I might take. This is why I call it camouflaged atheism. Saint Augustine was shrewd and prophetic when he said that a god who does not know the future is not God.

Here's the main thing: This kind of thinking fits nicely into a "name it and claim it" perspective. It works perfectly if you take the view that God does not have a will of His own but answers prayer only if we "declare" something when we pray. This also plays into the prophets of our day who "declare" what they want to happen and call it God's will! So if they want a person to be elected, they stick to their guns and don't give up until the prayer is answered. Their big mistake is when they say that "God told me" this or that.

I fear it is only a matter of time before the prophetic movement within the charismatic movement destroys itself. But it will take the coming of Isaac—with an appreciation and understanding of the book of Romans—to reveal the folly of open theism. It is deadly and ungodly.

The issue is so important that the next chapter is devoted to the importance of the will of God. With the coming of Isaac, the Church will once again become preoccupied with the desire to affirm, understand, and see God's will—and glory.

And this is the confidence that we have toward him, that if we ask anything according to his will he hears us. And if we know that he hears us in whatever we ask, we know that we have the requests that we have asked of him.
—1 John 5:14-15

Many are the plans in the mind of a man, but it is the purpose of the Lord that will stand.
—Proverbs 19:21

If you seek nothing but the will of God, He will put you in the right place at the right time.
—Smith Wigglesworth

Chapter Seven

THE WILL OF GOD

God does have a will of His own. Otherwise, why would someone like David consult the priest to apply the *Urim* and *Thummim*? The purpose of the *Urim* and *Thummim* was to reveal the will of God. God knows what is best, what is right, and what is good. *"No good thing"* will He withhold from us (Ps. 84:11). He knows the next step forward that we should do (see Prov. 3:6). First seen in Exodus 28:30, exactly what the *Urim* and *Thummim* looked like and how it was always applied are not clear. It was part of the breastplate of the priest. Apparently, David would reach blindly into a pouch for a white stone or black stone to get God's opinion. For example, David would ask the priest, *"Shall I pursue after this band? Shall I overtake them?"* In that case, the answer was yes: *"Pursue, for you shall surely overtake"* (1 Sam. 30:7-8). This is how they would discover what God willed. The point is, it was ever and ever an assumption that *Yahweh—the Most High God—certainly does have a will for His people!*

That has not changed. God does not change (see Mal. 3:6). He is the same God! Open theism is the extreme opposite to a God of glory. The God of glory is a jealous God. The German theologian Ludwig

Fuererbach (1804–1872) said that "God" is nothing but man's projection upon the backdrop of the universe. People want to believe there is a God—one who will look after them and take them to Heaven. Here's the thing: Based upon Fuererbach's principle, *nobody* would ever—ever—think of a God of glory! The glory of God is the sum total of all of His attributes—being omniscient, omnipresent, omnipotent, sovereign, love, just, and a hater of sin. Stephen introduced his defense before the Sanhedrin with the phrase *"The God of glory"* (Acts 7:2).

I'm sorry, but many Christians today—Charismatics and evangelicals—know so little about a God of glory or the glory of God.

Part of the reason for the previous chapter and this chapter is to demonstrate further why I regard the emergence of open theism within the charismatic movement as the ugliest—and most dangerous—development of all. If open theism were true, there would be no guarantee that God wins in the end! According to the book of Revelation, Jesus Christ wins! This is why He is *"the first and the last"* (Rev. 1:17). This is why satan will be punished forever and ever (see Rev. 20:10).

I hold to a personal principle about accepting preaching invitations. I never invite myself—or even hint—to speak. Except for one time. A few years before retiring from Westminster, I was told that a group of charismatic leaders in London were going to bring a famous Canadian theologian to speak on open theism. They said that it was only to be a debate, and there would be other speakers. I stepped in: "I want to speak." They said, "Sure." But two weeks before the conference, they cancelled me. They weren't having a debate; they wanted to bring open theism to England. I was very disappointed. I knew the speaker and knew what he would say. He took questions. One was "If what you say is true, is it not possible that God would not win but lose in the end?" The speaker was flustered. He looked up at the ceiling, then at the floor. And finally he admitted that this was true but believed somehow God would win. This admission is a dead giveaway that open theism is absolutely contrary to the Bible.

THE WILL OF GOD AND PRAYER

Some say that the purpose of prayer is to change God's will, that if we are not trying to change God's will we are wasting our time in prayer.

Wrong. The purpose of prayer is (1) to increase our sense of fellowship with Him, (2) to ask God to act, and (3) to *discover* what His will is—*and then do it.* In the Lord's Prayer, Jesus told us to pray, *"Your will be done on earth as it is in heaven"* (Matt. 6:10). Some take this to mean that there should be no sickness on earth since there is no sickness in Heaven. *But neither will anybody die in Heaven!* The meaning of this petition—*"Your will be done on earth as it is in heaven"*—is that we pray we will do exactly what God has commanded from His throne in Heaven. There is no rebellion in Heaven. This means I must pray there will be no rebellion in me. The preponderant way sin is understood in the Hebrew Old Testament and the Greek New Testament is *rebellion.*

If you are determined to change God's will rather than accept it, is this not bordering on rebellion? Surely to pray, *"Your will be done on earth as it is in heaven,"* is accepting His will and not trying to change it. Answered prayer, according to John, comes by praying *according to His will*. This means God has a will; He has already decided what is best for us. To get your prayer answered, you need to be "heard." The Hebraic concept of hearing comes from the Hebrew word *shamar*—to hear. The word *shamar* is ambiguous: It means both to obey and to hear, as a parent will say to their child, "Did you hear me?" If God *hears* you, your prayer will be obeyed—answered.

The angel Gabriel said to Zechariah, *"Your prayer has been heard,"* although that prayer had been made some twenty years before (Luke 1:13)! Zechariah had prayed in the will of God years before but had no idea his prayer had been heard. In any case, if—a big if—we pray *"according to his will he hears us"* (1 John 5:14). If you don't pray according to God's will, you are not heard. But if you persist on getting your way, God *might* acquiesce, as He has been known to do, as when He granted the children of Israel's request *"but sent a wasting disease among them"* (Ps. 106:15).

Dear friend, be very slow to try to change God's will. You are implying that your wisdom is greater than His. After Job was dealt a major attack by satan (with God's permission), his comment was: *"The Lord gave, and the Lord has taken away; blessed be the name of the Lord"* (Job 1:21). And never forget what Job learned from all he went through: *"I know that you can do all things and that no purpose of yours can be thwarted"* (Job 42:2).

On the other hand, John poses the possibility that we might *"know that we have been heard"* (1 John 5:15). This is another big if—that is, if we know that He hears us. That means God is pleased to let you know in advance that your prayer will be answered! That is a wonderful outcome but does not happen every day. It did not happen to Zechariah. He had no idea his prayer had been heard. The apostle Paul said that he did not always know what to pray for but prayed in the Spirit. If we pray in the Spirit, we are assured of at least one thing: We are praying the will of God. This is another proof that God *has a will*. The Holy Spirit intercedes *"according to the will of God"* (Rom. 8:26-27).

The will of God and the glory of God are inseparable.

The Greek word for *glory* is *doxa*. The root meaning of *doxa* is "opinion." The Hebrew word is *kabodh*—meaning "weight." We refer to "a prestigious or weighty person" or one who "throws his weight around." The God of glory has prestige and weight than which no greater can be conceived. The God of glory has an opinion and highly values His opinion.

The Most High God has dignity. His will has dignity. We sometimes forget that God has an opinion on things. He has an opinion on everything! The problem is, we don't always want His opinion! So what we do is decide what *we* want—and claim it as *His* will. Such thinking is totally foreign to the God of the Bible.

TWO LEVELS OF GOD'S WILL

There are two levels of God's will: His revealed will and His secret will. The revealed will may be seen in the Ten Commandments and the Sermon on the Mount. His revealed will is the content of the gospel of Jesus Christ. His revealed will is seen in justification by faith, salvation through the blood of Jesus, faith and repentance in order to receive the gospel. His revealed will is that Jesus is the God-man. Jesus was man as though He were not God; He was God as though He were not man. *"In the beginning was the Word, and the Word was with God, and the Word was God.... And the Word became flesh and dwelt among us, and we have seen his glory, glory as of the only Son from the father, full of grace and truth"* (John 1:1, 14). Jesus was born of a virgin, lived sinlessly on earth, died on a cross for our sins, was raised from the dead, ascended into Heaven, and is seated at the right hand of God where He ever lives to make intercession for us. The revealed will of God is that Jesus is coming again, that He will be the Supreme Judge, and that we all must stand before the judgment seat of Christ to give an account of the things done in the body (see 2 Cor. 5:10). The revealed will of God is the sixty-six books of the Bible. The revealed will of God are the four Gospels and the Epistles of Paul, James, Peter, and Jude.

In the revealed will of God, there is contained the truth of the secret will of God. It is known only to God unless He reveals it to us. The prophets revealed God's secret will. The Old Testament prophets foretold the coming of Jesus. There are canonical prophets and non-canonical prophets. The canonical prophets had books named after them—like Isaiah, Jeremiah, Ezekiel, Daniel, Zechariah, and Malachi. The non-canonical prophets did not have books named after them but were mightily used of God—like Nathan, Gad, Elijah, and Elisha. All of the prophets had in common that they spoke infallibly for God—some forecasting the future, some forecasting things going on in their own day. What must never be forgotten is that *the secret will of God never conflicts with the revealed will of God.* All the prophets represented the God of glory—a God of truth, love, holiness, and justice.

The secret will of God often deals with practical issues for God's people—whether one should get married, whether to take a certain job, what is one's calling, or what will happen in the future. God knows the future, *"declaring the end from the beginning"* (Isa. 46:10). That is how we know that Jesus is the *"first and the last."*

Many of us often get more interested in the secret will of God than the revealed will of God. The secret will of God often refers to the future. We ask, "What will I do? Where will I be?" We sadly sometimes forget to ask, "What pleases Him?"

In any case, God has a will of His own. He does not consult with us as to what to do! He knows what to do. He does not learn from us. He is not enriched by His creation. Of His own will He *"created the heavens and the earth"* (Gen. 1:1). There was a time before creation when there was nothing but God. If there had been one speck of dust in remotest space before creation, God would not have been first. Matter is not eternal. God created everything *ex nihilo*—"out of nothing."

THE WILL OF GOD AND PROPHECY

The apostle Peter referred to prophecy like this:

> *Knowing this first of all, that no prophecy of Scripture comes from someone's own interpretation. For no prophecy was ever produced by the will of man, but men spoke from God as they were carried along by the Holy Spirit* (2 Peter 1:20-21).

A prophet did not tell God what to do—or what God ought to do. A true prophet was concerned only with one thing: speaking what was on God's heart at the time. That might refer to the present; it could refer to the future. If God did not know the future, prophecy is not possible. Indeed, prophecy assumes that God knows what is needed for the present and what we ought to know about the future. As George Beverly Shea (1909–2013) once said, "Don't worry about the future; God has already been there."

> "I am the Alpha and the Omega," says the Lord God, "who is and who was and who is to come, the Almighty" (Revelation 1:8).

TRUE PROPHECY AND FALSE PROPHECY

I must add, when Peter said that *"no prophecy was ever produced by the will of man,"* he meant *true prophecy.* There are true prophets and false prophets. True prophets are genuine gold and faithful men and women of God. They not only have a "gift"; they have an unfeigned, abiding, and continual relationship with the Holy Spirit of God. They are pure, obedient, and reliable. But they are few, I'm afraid.

Jeremiah had a thorn in the flesh to contend with—a man named Hananiah. The situation was the bondage of Israel in Babylon. All the Israelites wanted to go home—to Jerusalem. A prophet named Hananiah told them what they wanted to hear: The captivity would last only two years. You can imagine how popular he was! But Jeremiah said, in so many words, "Sorry," that the exile would last seventy years (see Jer. 29:10). Jeremiah was not loved. He was not popular. But he got it right.

People for some reason—to this day—aspire to prophets who excite them and make them feel good. If a man can call out a person's birth date or street address, people go wild. Even if one said at the onslaught of COVID-19 in its early days that it was nothing to worry about—as one did in March 2020—and got it completely wrong, does the false prophet apologize? No. Do the people stop listening to him? No. We will want to feel good and get a word that makes us feel good—even if it's wrong.

It is not unlike people who consult their astrology chart even though it disappoints again and again. Or those who consult a medium who keeps disappointing. A lying spirit to a prophet can make some feel good. But the Elijahs and Elishas of this world refuse to do that. So, too, with Jeremiah. I will add that it is the Hananiahs of this world— and there were many—who in 2020 said that Donald Trump would be reelected for a second term in the 2020 election. It is what many wanted to hear. I too voted for Trump, by the way. I was disappointed. But a greater disappointment is that we do not seem to have the gen- uine Jeremiahs, Elijahs, and Elishas of this world around us. This (in my opinion) is another evidence that the charismatic movement is Ishmael. But Isaac is coming!

THE PURPOSE OF PROPHECY

The purpose of prophecy is to mirror the will of God. It is because God has a specific will for His people that prophecy exists. He chooses people to deliver His word. Generally speaking, prophecy pertains either to the present or the future. In many cases, prophecies that we may think pertain only to the future actually pertain to the present. God can kill two birds with one stone!

When the Messiah—called the Word—was in eternity before He took on a body, He said,

> *Behold, I have come; in the scroll of the book it is written of me: I delight to do your will, O my God* (Psalm 40:7-8).
>
> *A body have you prepared for me.... Behold, I have come to do your will, O God, as it is written of me in the scroll of the book* (Hebrews 10:5-7).

Jesus did not come to change the will of God; He came to do the will of God because the Father had a work for Jesus to accomplish. If anybody could have changed the will of the Father, it would have been Jesus. But no. In Gethsemane, He prayed, *"Father, if you are willing, remove this cup from me. Nevertheless, not my will, but yours, be done"* (Luke 22:42).

THE WILL OF GOD AND PAIN

When Jesus prayed as He did in Gethsemane, it was because He wanted to avoid pain. Physical pain. Emotional pain. Spiritual pain. It is the most natural thing in the world to want to avoid pain. Loneliness. Withheld vindication. Financial worries. Being misunderstood. Being hated. Sudden disappointment. The list is endless.

Why is this section of the present book important? Answer: the five wise virgins in Matthew 25:1-6 had oil in their vessels. The oil is a symbol of the Spirit. When Samuel poured oil on David, the Spirit of God came suddenly on David (see 1 Sam. 16:13). The coming of Isaac will be a joining together of the Word and the Spirit. As I said, we honor the Spirit by esteeming the Spirit's greatest product—the Bible. We learn in Scripture how God's sovereign vessels experienced suffering. Abraham. Isaac. Jacob. Joseph. Moses. Samuel and all those listed in Hebrews 11. Away with the notion that, "if the apostle Paul had my faith, he would not have had his thorn in the flesh." Such nonsense—what I might call the essence of "Ishmaelite thinking"—has drawn people away from Holy Scripture and encouraged them to think of only what "feels good."

When we take oil in our vessels, we experience the Holy Spirit. We then are able to find out what grieves the Spirit and what pleases Him (see Eph. 4:30-32; 5:10). We learn to give thanks. We learn to accept that we must not only believe on Christ but suffer for Him, that we are *"destined"* for afflictions (see Phil 1:29; 1 Thess. 3:3). This means that, when the "midnight cry" comes, we are the ones who will be used of God in the coming revival.

That means *now* is the time of testing. How we face testing now, how we face trials now, how we accept vindication withheld now, and how we cope with loneliness and disappointment now. My friend Arthur Blessitt always said, "Circumstances don't change the commitment." Two days before Christmas 1966, Arthur was told, "You have an aneurism in your brain. You must not move." On Christmas Day 1966, he discharged himself from the hospital and began his walk from Hollywood, California. He made a commitment to begin his walk on Christmas Day. He is still alive (and still has the aneurism) and is mentioned in the *Guinness Book of Records* that he has the record for the longest walk in the world (over 40,000 miles).

Arthur Blessitt turned us upside down at Westminster Chapel when I invited him to preach for us six Sunday nights in April through May of 1982. It was the best decision I made in twenty-five years there. He is a man of the Word. He challenged us to the hilt to believe the Bible—about witnessing and the glory of the Lord.

When Isaac comes, there will be a general turning to the Bible. But those who know their Bibles will be the ones used of the Lord. Jesus promised that one of the things the Holy Spirit would do would be to remind one of what Jesus taught (see John 14:26). We may ask, "What is the importance of reading your Bible? Why go to Bible study—it is so boring? Why read the book of Romans and especially Romans chapter four?" The answer is, we will be *reminded* of what we have sought to know! If there is nothing to be reminded of, how can the Holy Spirit remind you? Will the Holy Spirit just pour Romans 4 into your mind? I don't think so. In a word, if we are empty-headed when the Spirit falls on us, we will be empty-headed afterward! Now is the time to prepare for the coming move of God.

In a word, how we react to pain, to suffering, and to the call to know more of God's Word is important.

When the three kings from the east came into Jerusalem—the first great awakening—it got everybody to turn to the Scriptures to see where Messiah would be born (see Matt. 2:1-6). People were shaken to their fingertips. The coming of Isaac will do the same and result in a turning to the Bible. In the Great Reformation of the sixteenth century, there was a turning to the Bible. The printing press made copies of the Bible. The world was turned upside down.

That will happen again—except there will be no more need of the printing press. People have Bibles in their homes—on coffee tables, on shelves. But people don't read them! Those who know their Bibles will receive the tap of God on their shoulders, saying, "I have a special work for you to do before the end." The teaching of the Bible is what matters. What does the Bible say? It is the only thing that matters.

By the way, as we will see in the following pages, I hope God will use *you* in the coming great move of God.

But at midnight [middle of night; Gr.: meses de nuktos] *there was a cry, "Here is the bridegroom! Come out to meet him." Then all those virgins rose and trimmed their lamps.*

—Matthew 25:6-7

For still the vision awaits its appointed time; it hastens to the end—it will not lie. If it seems slow, wait for it; it will surely come; it will not delay.

—Habakkuk 2:3

It ain't over till it's over.

—Yogi Berra (1925–2015)

Chapter Eight

THE MIDNIGHT CRY

The next thing to happen on God's calendar is not the second coming of Jesus but the awakening of the Church *just before* the second coming. I believe the coming of Isaac—when the Word and the Spirit finally come together—is eschatological. The word *eschatology* comes from the Greek word *eschatos,* which means "last things." This means we are talking about "end of the world" stuff—what happens just before the end.

I believe it is both the final outpouring of the Holy Spirit before the end, but also very near.

A crucial question, therefore, you have probably been asking is this: Is the next great move of God the final move of God just before the end, or is the next great move of God merely another needed awakening of the Church? I believe that it is the fulfillment of the midnight cry as in the parable of the ten virgins. *I hold that the coming of Isaac is the final move of God in the world before the actual second coming of Jesus Christ.*

The Old Testament canonical prophet Habakkuk wanted to know why God allowed suffering (see Hab. 1:2-4). God told him to station himself on a tower. Habakkuk believed the Lord would reveal why God has allowed evil, injustice, and suffering. But when Habakkuk stationed himself on the tower, it seemed that God was kicking a can down the road—only to put off revealing what Habakkuk so desperately wanted to know. But God did speak to Habakkuk, only to say that the answer would be revealed in *"the end"*—the last day. The reason *why God allows evil* is called a *"vision."* Habakkuk was told that it would be a long time before the end. It would seem that Habakkuk wrote this in approximately 600 BC. If so, Habakkuk was told this some 2,700 years ago. That's a long time. And when God said that the *"vision"* would tarry, that it would *"seem slow"* or delayed, we would have to agree! In a word, God was implying to Habakkuk that the end would come, but Habakkuk would not get his answer soon. Habakkuk must wait—a long time.

Habakkuk might have angrily said, "That's not good enough; I want to know right now." But if that reaction had crossed his mind, we can safely say he calmed down. Because the book of Habakkuk ends with this:

> *Though the fig tree should not blossom, nor fruit be on the vines, the produce of the olive fail and the fields yield no food, the flock be cut off from the fold and there be no herd in the stalls, yet I will rejoice in the Lord; I will take joy in the God of my salvation* (Habakkuk 3:17-18).

WHAT ABRAHAM AND HABAKKUK HAD IN COMMON

When God told Abraham—aged 85, Sarah 75—that he would have a son, Abraham might have said, "Do you expect me to believe that?" But he believed it. And God counted him as righteous (see Gen. 15:6). When God told Habakkuk that the reason God allows suffering would be revealed on the last day and not immediately, Habakkuk accepted it (see Hab. 3:17–19). We may be sure that God counted Habakkuk as righteous! There followed the quote *"The righteous shall live by his faith"* (Hab. 2:4). The reason is this: If Abraham could be counted righteous by believing the promise, so too Habakkuk would be counted righteous by waiting until the last day for God to clear His name.

This statement—*"the righteous shall live by his faith"*—is quoted three times in the New Testament. But in the New Testament it is related more to Abraham's faith than to Habakkuk's. The statement *"The righteous will live by his faith"* is quoted by the apostle Paul two times regarding his teaching of justification by faith alone and once by the writer to the Hebrews (see Rom. 1:17; Gal. 3:11). The writer to the Hebrews quotes it to encourage Christian Jews who were on the verge of giving up (see Heb. 10:38).

There are two things implied in this statement that might be unnoticed: (1) the Hebrew word for *"faith"* means "faithfulness," and (2) the *"his"* in Habakkuk 2:4 refers to *God's faithfulness*. It, therefore, means the righteous shall live by the faithfulness of God. A commentary found in the Dead Sea Scrolls shows that this is the way Jewish scholars interpreted it. Indeed, this is exactly the way the writer to the Hebrews interpreted it in Hebrews 10:38. The writer to the Hebrews encouraged discouraged Christian Jews not to give up: *"Do not throw away your confidence," "you have need of endurance," "you may receive what is promised,"* in a little while *"the coming one will come and will not delay; but my righteous one will live by faith"* (Heb. 10:35-37).

In other words, *we must have faith in the faithfulness of God*; the writer urges Hebrew Christians to live by the faithfulness of God to keep His word. Those who live by the faithfulness of God are imputed with righteousness—as Abraham was.

The apostle Paul quoted Habakkuk 2:4 twice regarding the teaching of justification by faith (see Rom. 1:17; Gal. 3:11). Whereas Paul referred to Abraham's faith, the quotation comes from Habakkuk! This is why we must compare Abraham and Habakkuk. Since Habakkuk 2:4 is quoted in the New Testament with reference to justification by faith, the context of Habakkuk 2:4 refers to the prophet having to wait long before the "vision" of *why God allows suffering* to be unfolded. Habakkuk was saying in so many words: One day, God will clear His name.

God is the most hated person in the universe. People accuse God—"if indeed He exists"—for all the troubles of the world. People say that God has a lot to answer for. One day, God *will* reveal why He has allowed evil and suffering over the ages. In Habakkuk, it is called a *"vision."* God will reveal what is true. Those who shake their fists at God in the meantime will never be justified. But those who will wait for the vision—that is, wait until the end—will be regarded as righteous in God's eyes. In other words, we as Bible believers must vindicate God *now!* When *"every knee"* shall bow and *"every tongue confess that Jesus Christ is Lord,"* it will be a glorious vindication for those of us who affirm God now as a God of justice and love (Phil. 2:9-11).

The midnight cry will precipitate the next great move of God. The midnight cry gets things moving. The midnight cry shows that the end is nigh. The midnight cry will awaken the Church. The midnight cry will expose who is spiritual and who isn't. The midnight cry will lead to the fulfillment of Habakkuk's promise, *"The earth will be filled with the knowledge of the glory of the Lord as the waters cover the sea"* (Hab. 2:14). The midnight cry will not only restore the message of the second coming but will cause people everywhere to realize that Jesus is coming soon. As fear came upon every soul on the Day of Pentecost, so will there be a restoration of the fear of God in the Church and the world, too.

A VERY IMPORTANT DISTINCTION

But note that the midnight cry and the second coming are separated. All I say about the coming of Isaac and revival before the end hangs on this. The cry and the second coming do not come at once. If the second coming of Jesus came simultaneously with the midnight cry, there could be no conversation between the wise and the foolish virgins. I say this because, as soon as they heard the midnight cry, *"the foolish said to the wise, 'Give us some of your oil, for our lamps are going out'"* (Matt. 25:8). How could they say this if Jesus had come in glory? It would be over then! *"But the wise answered, saying, 'Since there will*

163

not be enough for us and for you, go rather to the dealers and buy for yourselves' (Matt. 25:9). This shows a time period between the cry in the middle of the night and the moment when the Bridegroom indeed comes.

Many of us have assumed that midnight meant twelve o'clock midnight. I used to think this as well. The word *midnight* comes from three Greek words—*meses de nuktos*—that mean "middle of night." In other words, the cry that Jesus is coming soon will take place when nobody expects it! Picture yourself asleep at two o'clock in the morning! The midnight cry will awaken the Church when nobody anticipates it—when we are not in the least expecting anything to happen.

Jesus introduced the parable of the ten virgins in Matthew 25:1 (NIV) with the word "Then," or *"At that time."* He had just been talking about the very last days in Matthew 24. Remember that there were no chapters and verses in the original Greek. Matthew continued to speak about the very last days and then said, *"At that time,"* meaning that the Church will be asleep in the last days. I think that the best description of the modern Church is that it is asleep, speaking spiritually. That is the way the ten virgins are described: *"As the bridegroom was delayed, they all became drowsy and slept"* (Matt. 25:5).

Here are three things about sleep: (1) you don't know you were asleep until you wake up, (2) you do things in your sleep you would not do if wide awake, and (3) you hate the sound of an alarm. We much prefer to roll over and sleep on. But in the middle of the night, there was a cry. The cry was *"Here is the bridegroom!"*

THE ANCIENT MIDDLE EASTERN WEDDING

Jesus was referring to the ancient Middle Eastern wedding. His hearers would have possibly understood the parable better than you and I can. Here is partly what we know about the typical ancient Middle Eastern wedding. It could last seven days. The wedding did not take place in a church or a synagogue but in the bridegroom's home. The bride would wait in her home for the bridegroom to come and get her. The bride would have female attendants who carried lamps to give illumination when it was dark. This is because, strange as it may seem to us, the bridegroom would sometimes come in the middle of the night! The bride and her attendants were required to be ready because they did not know for sure when the bridegroom would come for his bride. That is the background for this parable; the bridegroom is Jesus:

> *Then the kingdom of heaven will be like ten virgins who took their lamps and went to meet the bridegroom. Five of them were foolish, and five were wise. For when the foolish took their lamps, they took no oil with them, but the wise took flasks of oil with their lamps. As the bridegroom was delayed, they all became drowsy and slept. But at midnight [middle of the night] there was a cry, "Here is the bridegroom! Come out to meet him." Then all those virgins rose and trimmed their lamps. And the foolish said to the wise, "Give us some of your oil, for our lamps are going out." But the wise answered, saying, "Since there will not be enough for us and for you, go rather to the dealers and*

buy for yourselves." And while they were going to buy, the bridegroom came, and those who were ready went in with him to the marriage feast, and the door was shut. Afterward the other virgins came also, saying, "Lord, lord, open to us." But he answered, "Truly, I say to you, I do not know you." Watch therefore for you know neither the day nor the hour (Matthew 25:1-13).

Here in brief is the meaning of the parable of the ten virgins:

1. The Church may be described in the last days as sleep.

2. The Church here is depicted as *"wise"* and *"foolish"* virgins.

3. The wise had ample oil (Holy Spirit); the foolish did not have enough.

4. The cry came in the middle of the night, meaning when nobody expected it.

5. The Church was awakened.

6. The foolish realized they were in deep trouble and begged the wise for help.

7. The wise instructed the foolish to get more oil, that is, call on God.

8. But while the foolish were doing this, Jesus came—that is, the second coming.

9. The marriage feast followed; only the wise could enjoy it.

10. We are told to be ready since we do not know when this will happen.

It is my view that the next great move of God is described in this parable. *"Lamps"* may refer to the Word. *"Your word is a lamp to my feet and a light to my path"* (Ps. 119:105). As we have seen, the oil refers to the Spirit. This parable shows the Word and Spirit.

The next great move of God—if we follow the parable—takes place *after* the awakening in the middle of the night and *before* the coming of the Bridegroom. How long this lasts, I do not know. Days? Months? A year or two? I am not prepared to say.

It will come suddenly. It will be a great awakening. "Death is the final wake-up call," as Douglas Horton (1891–1968) put it. But the midnight cry will be a wake-up call that precedes death. And yet it is "over" for the foolish. Yogi Berra said, "It ain't over till it's over." It is not over for the reader of this book; I wish this book to be a wake-up call to prepare us. Indeed, it will lead to the next great move of God on this planet. And if I have interpreted correctly, this move of God will lead to *"the knowledge of the glory of the Lord"* covering the earth *"as the waters cover the sea."* Millions will be saved.

For the person described as *"foolish"* in the parable of the ten virgins, it was, sadly, over. The door was *"shut"* when they tried to get into the marriage feast. This is a warning to those who have not taken the Holy Spirit seriously enough. I am *not* saying or implying that cessationists typify the foolish virgins. But all Christians should take this word very seriously. If my book serves to give cessationists pause, good!

I also believe the blindness that has come upon Israel for over two thousand years will be lifted. I believe that the Word and Spirit coming together will precipitate what I have stated.

"ONE MORE THING"

There is "one more thing," as Columbo would say. Three groups are implied in the parable of the ten virgins: (1) the wise, (2) the foolish, (are you ready for this?) and (3) *preachers*—not necessarily ordained or very educated—who are actively involved in the midnight cry.

Who, then, calls out, *"Here is the bridegroom!"*—an angel? Or a person? Those who actually participate in the midnight cry are *not asleep*. Whereas I am sure that the Church, speaking generally, is asleep, there are those who have faithfully upheld the need for both the Word and Spirit. They are unknown but faithful Bible believers. This will include those never ordained and or seminary educated. They will get the tap on the shoulder and be right in the middle of the next great move of God. There will be no superstars. Ordinary people who are knowledgeable in the Word and trusted with the gifts of the Holy Spirit will be preaching, healing, and mightily used of God.

Reader, that could be you.

*Who will roll away the stone for us
from the entrance of the tomb?*
—Mark 16:3

*The burden that once I carried is gone,
is gone Of all of my sins there remaineth not
one, not one; Jesus, the Saviour has ransomed
me, Bearing my sins upon Calvary, Giving me
glorious liberty, The burden of sin is gone.*
—Haldor Lillenas (1885–1959)

Chapter Nine

HOW WILL WE RECOGNIZE
THE COMING OF ISAAC?

No one saw the resurrection of Jesus. There were no BBC cameras stationed at the tomb of Jesus to record the entire episode so that the world would believe it happened.

Was anyone required to bring about the resurrection of Jesus from the dead?

No. Three women hurried to the tomb of Jesus on Easter morning but suddenly panicked: *"Who will roll away the stone?"* they said. They should have thought of that! They were not expecting an empty tomb; they came to anoint the body of Jesus. But, lo and behold, the stone was already rolled away! In other words, the burden that they carried on the way to the tomb was gone when they arrived! I cannot help but think of an old song I used to hear as a boy: "The burden that once I carried is gone, is gone" ("My Burden Is Gone," Haldor Lillenas).

As I write this book, the silly thought crosses my mind, *Do I need to make the next great move of God happen?* Of course not. This is God's problem!

Even if you believe what has been written in this book, do you and I have a responsibility to bring about the next great move of God? The answer is, it is out of our hands.

It will be like the falling of the Spirit on the Day of Pentecost. What was required? Waiting. They were obeying the last words of Jesus before He ascended to the right hand of God.

They might have anticipated that receiving power from upon high would have taken place on an important day like Pentecost—fifty days after Passover. It did. But they did not think of that until it happened. It came *"suddenly"* (Acts 2:2). One might say they should not have been surprised. But they were.

THERE MUST HAVE BEEN A PLAN

I think of verses such as these:

> *The time that the people of Israel lived in Egypt was 430 years. At the end of 430 years, on that very day, all the hosts of the Lord went out from the land of Egypt* (Exodus 12:40-41).

> *So all the generations from Abraham to David were fourteen generations, and from David to the deportation to Babylon fourteen generations, and from the deportation to Babylon to the Christ fourteen generations* (Matthew 1:17).

> *But when the fulness of time had come, God sent forth his Son, born of woman, born under the law, to redeem those*

*who were under the law, so that we might receive adoption
as sons* (Galatians 4:4-5).

Verses like these make one see that there must have been a plan.
To God, it was advanced knowledge. But to us it was *a posteriori* as
an adverb—what is based on knowledge *after* the event. Nothing took
God by surprise. Nothing *ever* takes God by surprise. But it may take
us by surprise. The words *"on that very day,"* the reference to *"fourteen
generations,"* and the phrase *"fulness of time"* lead us to believe that the
day and hour of the midnight cry, *too,* is set in time. We are specifically
told that the *"day and hour"* of the second coming is known of the
Father (Matt. 24:36). It shows that God knows the future. It, therefore, should not have been a surprise that Jesus' words *"You will receive
power"* were fulfilled on the Day of Pentecost—on schedule (Acts 1:8).

But they were surprised.

Will the coming of Isaac be like Pentecost? I believe so. It is possible that, in Heaven, we will learn *a posteriori* that the midnight cry
came like other previously mentioned events. But Pentecost came as a
surprise, and it came to a few. And yet it led to three thousand conversions to Jesus Christ within hours. It eventually spread throughout
Jerusalem and all Israel—eventually the world.

The Christian faith had small beginnings. *"For whoever has despised
the day of small things shall rejoice"* (Zech. 4:10). A virgin became
pregnant in Nazareth. A baby named Jesus was born in Bethlehem.
The first announcement of it came to shepherds. It culminated in the
crucifixion of the same Jesus thirty-three years later. This was initially
seen as a gross disappointment. The resurrection of Jesus took place
with no witnesses.

It was the *preaching of the gospel* that convinced people that Jesus was raised from the dead, not a miracle or a healing. *"It pleased God through the folly of what we preach to save those who believe"* (1 Cor. 1:21).

Preaching is God's method. Always has been, always will be.

The disciples' job was to convince unbelieving Jews that Jesus of Nazareth had been raised from the dead. I repeat: It was not miracles before peoples' eyes that led to three thousand baptisms that did it. It was not people being healed that did it. It was not apologetics that did it. It was not learned, educated men that persuaded them. It was those who *"had been with Jesus"* (Acts 4:13). It was the Word and the Spirit that did it. It was the immediate presence of the Spirit along with Peter's words that caused astonished men to ask, *"What shall we do?"* The bottom line: It was the preaching of the gospel through the power of the Holy Spirit that did it.

Miracles came later. Healings came later. People being delivered from demons came later.

It began with one hundred and twenty men and women who were filled with the Holy Spirit. They—ordinary people—were the ones who shook people rigid in Jerusalem on the Day of Pentecost. The first reaction of those who observed them was to mock them. *"They are filled with new wine"* (Acts 2:13). Someone had to explain what was happening. Peter stood up and explained what was happening. It was the fulfillment of Old Testament verses:

> *"And in the last days it shall be, God declares, that I will pour out my Spirit on all flesh, and your sons and your*

daughters shall prophesy, and your young men shall see visions, and your old men shall dream dreams... (Acts 2:17; Joel 2:28).

Peter then applied words from the psalmist David:

I saw the Lord always before me, for he is at my right hand that I may not be shaken; therefore my heart is glad and my flesh also will dwell in hope. For you will not abandon my soul to Hades, or let your Holy One see corruption. You have made known to me the paths of life; you will make me full of gladness with your presence (Acts 2:25-28; Psalm 16:8-11).

After that Peter quoted another psalm: *"The Lord said to my Lord, 'Sit at my right hand until I make your enemies your footstool'"* (Acts 2:34; Ps. 110:1).

It was the Scriptures and the power of God that did it.

It was the early disciples' job, then, to explain that Jesus was raised from the dead. They had their work cut out for them. How could they explain that Jesus was alive and well when Jesus was not around? Where was He? Why should people believe such an extraordinary claim?

SMALL BEGINNINGS

The Christian faith continued to have small beginnings. The sight of an empty tomb did not thrill the three women who came to anoint

Jesus' body. But one of those three women refused to leave. It was Mary Magdalene. She thought at first she saw the gardener. The tomb was in a garden. But she recognized a voice who called her name: *"Mary."* That voice had changed her life. That very voice made seven demons leave her. That voice came from a man who gave her love and respect. The first person to see the risen Jesus was Mary Magdalene. Small beginnings.

Word spread to the eleven disciples. For some forty days, Jesus would show up—then disappear. The disciples were perplexed. Peter announced, *"I am going fishing"* (John 21:3). A few others followed. Jesus ate fish before them. He lovingly lectured Peter, forcing Peter to see for himself that he did not love Jesus as much as he once thought. Eventually, five hundred people saw the risen Jesus (see 1 Cor. 15:6).

BIG BUT ILL-POSED QUESTION

But there was a burning question on the disciples' minds. They were frustrated. They believed that Jesus was raised from the dead but did not know why. Or even why He died. The problem was, they never grasped His teaching that the Kingdom of God was not visible (see Luke 17:20). They believed all along that the Messiah would overthrow Rome—and that Jesus was the Anointed One who would do precisely that. But this was not happening. It did not happen on Palm Sunday. Their hopes were dashed when He was crucified—and really died.

However, Jesus' resurrection raised their hopes. But why didn't He start doing this? Why appear and disappear? They had one question on their minds: *"Lord, will you at this time restore the kingdom to Israel?"* (Acts 1:6). This shows that Jesus' teaching on the Kingdom of God, all the parables, the Sermon on the Mount, and the teaching about "another" Helper coming had not penetrated their minds. Jesus disappointed them when He said it was *"not for you to know times or seasons that the Father has fixed by his own authority"* (Acts 1:7). He had basically one word for them: *"Wait."* Wait in Jerusalem so that they would receive *"power from on high"* (Luke 24:49). Indeed, *"You will receive power when the Holy Spirit has come upon you, and you will be my witnesses in Jerusalem and in all Judea and Samaria, and to the end of the earth"* (Acts 1:8).

What they would later realize was that Jesus was helping them to make the transition from the level of nature to the level of the Spirit. This process may have started when He *"breathed"* on them and said, *"Receive the Holy Spirit"* (John 20:22). They would need another ten days to absorb what Jesus said to them before He ascended to Heaven. Perhaps the teaching of the parables began to sink in. The meaning of the Kingdom. And the purpose of all of Jesus' teachings.

THE SPIRIT MADE THE DIFFERENCE

But when the Spirit fell on them on the Day of Pentecost, they finally got it! They would no doubt continue to learn. But it was clear enough to Peter that he spoke with power, authority, and persuasion that went way beyond the level of nature. The cowardly Peter who denied Jesus a few weeks before was utterly fearless before thousands of people (see John 18:25-27). Instead of him being afraid of the people, the people were afraid of him. Three thousand were saved the first day. The Holy Spirit convinced the three thousand that Jesus was alive indeed and reigning from the right hand of God!

In a word, the Spirit of God made Jesus as real at the level of the Spirit as He had previously been at the level of nature.

How does this relate to the next great move of God? First, the cry in the middle of the night will come to some believers somewhere in the world. I don't know where. It could be Britain. It could be America. It could be Australia. It could be Moscow. It could be Beijing. It could be Hong Kong. It will make world news in a single day.

What will do it? Preaching.

Who will do it? Those who announce the coming of the Bridegroom.

It will awaken the Church—the wise and the foolish—all over the world as it spreads from one location to another. It will eventually touch the entire world. As God chose Jerusalem as the place of beginning, He will choose a place for the initial hearing of the midnight cry. The glory of the Lord will eventually cover the earth *"as the waters cover the sea."*

There are, therefore, *three* groups of people described in Matthew 25:1-13: (1) the wise virgins; (2) the foolish virgins; and (3) those who participate in the midnight cry, saying, *"Here is the bridegroom! Come out to meet him!"* (Matt. 25:6). The same power that will awaken the local church that God chooses will spread throughout the world. The same level of power that fell on the one hundred and twenty on the

Day of Pentecost will spread from city to city, nation to nation, and reach the entire world. It took months and a few years for the gospel originally to spread throughout Judea and Samaria and the Grae-co-Roman world. But with television and the internet, the same power that raised Jesus from the dead will spread throughout the world in a very short period of time, possibly only days. When the Passover in Hezekiah's day *"came about suddenly,"* how much more will the power of God spread in our day (2 Chron. 29:36)!

Then the miracles will follow. People will be raised from the dead as in the book of Acts. The same power that healed the forty-year-old man who never walked will heal crippled people in every nation. The same power that struck Ananias and Sapphira dead for their hypocrisy will precipitate a fear of God everywhere that has not been seen before. People who seemed unreachable—whether from liberal pulpits, the mafia, politicians, a biased media, and the poorest of the poor—will be suddenly converted like Saul of Tarsus.

But not all will be saved. Not all will be healed. Not all will be struck dead. But all will be witnesses to the power of the living God. The name of Jesus will be extolled. The glory of the name of the Lord will be restored.

It will all begin with the preaching of the gospel—the historic gospel will be vindicated. The teaching of justification as in Romans 4 will prevail everywhere. Cessatonism, open theism, denial of the Bible, upholding of abortion, same sex marriage, and corrupt TV preachers who consistently ask for money will be exposed. Racism and corruption in politics, education, and the financial system will be exposed and put to open shame.

It will have small beginnings. It could begin with a Mary Magdalene. It could begin with a small group—a dozen, a hundred and twenty, or more.

Where? I have no idea. When? Soon. When the wise and foolish are in a deep, deep sleep, expecting nothing. As Peter said, *"This is that,"* so will you the reader say, "This is it" (Acts 2:16—various versions).

No one will need to tell you. Most of all, the God of the Bible will have the last word.

Prepare to meet your God, O Israel.
—Amos 4:12

*Most people don't like change. They revolt against
it unless they can clearly see the advantage it
brings. For that reason, when good leaders prepare
to take action or make changes, they take people
through a process to get them ready for it.*
—John C. Maxwell

Chapter Ten

PREPARATION FOR ISAAC

Change is coming. Big change. But we cannot hasten it. Neither can we stop it.

With one exception, there is no way to prepare for it.

What might that exception be? Who might it be?

You. Yes, you, hopefully, the reader of this book. That is what this final chapter is about. I choose to believe that *you,* the reader of this book—at least some of you—are to be compared to the one hundred and twenty people on the Day of Pentecost. It came to people, ordinary, not extraordinary, human beings.

As the Spirit of God on the Day of Pentecost came suddenly, so the midnight cry will come suddenly. As the falling of the Spirit fell on a few—one hundred and twenty men and women who were ready and waiting—so will the next great move of God begin with a few. That is, what this chapter is about. This sudden awakening will come:

- when the Church generally—not to mention the world— least *expects* it;

- when the Church least *wants* it;
- when the Church is least *prepared* for it.

Remember, too, that the midnight cry comes in *mestes de nuktos* (Gr. literally, "middle of night")—that is, metaphorically speaking. It will come when no one is thinking about it.

As I stated previously, there are three groups described in Matthew 25:1-13. They are: (1) the wise virgins, (2) the foolish virgins, and (3) *preachers*—laymen and trained—who will actively participate in the midnight cry. It would not be edifying or profitable to enter into the issue whether the foolish virgins are saved or lost; I touch on this in my book *Prepare Your Heart for the Midnight Cry* (Charisma House). What is undoubtedly true is that the virgins represent the Church, speaking generally, whatever its state. Also, I would not suggest that five wise and five foolish virgins means 50 percent of the Church are wise and 50 percent are foolish. I have no idea what percentage we are writing about.

But I do believe this: The foolish will be painfully conscious of their spiritual failure. I can only imagine how this parable will be fulfilled by the foolish pleading with the wise, *"Give us some of your oil."* I would not be surprised if there will be those who beg for spiritual help and prayer during this great move of God but will be denied help. This sounds harsh. But it seems to me that the cry *"Here is the bridegroom"* will be oath-level clarity—indeed, an oath sworn in wrath. It will be too late for some people to enjoy the benefit of the move of God that will include signs, wonders, miracles, and countless conversions all over the globe.

THE THIRD GROUP: MESSENGERS

The third group are preachers: very possibly people who are laymen—but those who know their Bibles. Preachers—possibly many who have never been ordained—who are unashamed of the gospel! It is likely that some of these are not known as preachers or professional clergymen. They may be untrained. But they will be able to explain Romans 4.

There is a significant precedent for ordinary believers spreading the word. Furthermore, as there was persecution in the days of the earliest church, so too will there be hatred for the true gospel and hostility toward those who are unashamed of it. *"And there arose on that day a great persecution against the church in Jerusalem, and they were all scattered throughout the regions of Judea and Samaria, except the apostles"* (Acts 8:1). This demonstrates how the ordinary believers took over the task of spreading the gospel in the very early church.

I think of one of our deacons at Westminster Chapel, Bob George, also a Gideon, who responded to the call to be a soul-winner through the influence of Arthur Blessitt. Mr. George had boldness and fearlessness like no layman I have seen in my sixty-five years of ministry. He personally led over five hundred people in Buckingham Gate and Victoria to pray to receive Christ between 1982 and 2002. He was trained in a teaching method called Evangelism Explosion.

A New Pecking Order

On the other hand, I can envisage many professional ministers who turn to the Bible only when they need a sermon. I believe they will be like the foolish virgins who say to the wise virgins, *"Give us some of your oil."* The new move of God will reveal a new pecking order. The professionals, the high-profile Christian leaders and church members who have not been the slightest bit concerned for the lost, will be completely forgotten in this move of God. These are those to whom it will be said, *"I do not know you"* (Matt. 25:12).

What is the message of the midnight cry? Answer: the unchanging, eternal gospel. The message: *"Fear God and give him glory, because the hour of his judgment has come"* (Rev. 14:6-7). The message will not only be a restoration of the teaching of justification by faith alone but also accentuated by the unashamed truth that *Jesus is coming soon.* Virtually nobody believes this now. But they will then. The "eternal gospel" will shake rigid those who have had no fear of God. Such unbelief and scoffing about Bible teaching will change immediately. This power will be the immediate result of the Word and Spirit coming together. The simultaneous combination will result in spontaneous combustion. As people cried out to Peter, *"What shall we do?"* so will people everywhere cry out to the messengers who announce that Jesus is coming soon.

Whose voice is it, then, that will utter the cry in the middle of the night? Is it the voice of an angel? No. An archangel? No. A superstar? No. It will be *preachers*—ordinary people—who will be equipped by the power of the Spirit as the one hundred and twenty had—that Peter had. The raw power of God will enable trained and untrained ministers of the gospel to speak with boldness, fearlessness, and authority unlike anything witnessed in centuries.

NO SUPERSTARS

There will be no superstars in the next great move of God on the earth. No famous people will be announcing that Jesus is coming soon.

As God used fishermen, born-again tax collectors, and unheard-of followers of Jesus in the days of the early church, so will unknown servants of God speak with such power that countless people will fall to their knees asking, *"What shall we do?"*

How is this possible? The same Spirit of God that took a coward like Simon Peter to cause Jewish priests and politicians to marvel and be nervous and afraid, so will He take people like you who have believed the Bible and the God of the Bible over the years to demand the godless to repent.

Some of you reading this book will be right in the middle of the next great move of God. Some of you will stand where no person has stood since the days of the early church.

The midnight cry will be uttered by people who will have been empowered by the *spiritual* coming of Jesus that will awaken the Church prior to the second coming of Jesus. As for the second coming, it is the literal, physical coming of Jesus. It will be announced by an *archangel* when *"every eye shall see him,"* and people throughout the earth will wail because of Jesus (1 Thess. 4:16; see Rev. 1:7).

INSTANTANEOUS AND SPONTANEOUS

In a word, the midnight cry will be the instant and spontaneous consequence of the coming of the Spirit of God upon those who will deliver the message of the gospel and the soon coming of Jesus Himself. Sometime later—how long? Not long. The archangel with a voice as clear as the sound of a trumpet will introduce the coming of the Son of God. How much later? Time enough for millions to turn to the Lord Jesus Christ. But with the internet and television it could take a very short period of time. Time enough to demonstrate how those in the Church—called foolish virgins—are not granted true repentance. They will fulfill the pitiful words *"Give us some of your oil"* (Matt. 25:8). These are those who are not allowed into the marriage supper (see Matt. 25:7-13).

I have passed over eschatological details implied in the parable of the ten virgins. This book is largely about the coming of the Spirit that will awaken the Church and lead to the conversion of millions in the world. This will be the greatest revival in the history of the world. It will lead to the lifting of the blindness on the people of Israel—whether in Jerusalem, Tel Aviv, Golders Green in London, Brooklyn, Miami, or Los Angeles. It will result in the conversion of many Muslims—whether in the Middle East or the Far East. It will lead to conversions of Bhuddists in China, Japan, and other nations.

Not all will be saved. Not all were saved on or after the Day of Pentecost. Not all were saved in the Wesleyan revival of the eighteenth century. But many were saved. Not all were saved in the Welsh revival. But many were saved.

These things said, those who are chosen to utter the cry—*"Here is the bridegroom"* (ESV), *"Here's the bridegroom"* (NIV), or *"Behold, the bridegroom cometh"* (KJV)—are like the one hundred and twenty that waited for the Spirit to fall on the Day of Pentecost. Even they could not hasten the day; they had to wait. But they were aware it would be coming soon. They also need to be prepared as the one hundred and twenty were.

The people who will speak with an authority that has not been heard for many a generation *"Here's the bridegroom,"* which awakened the ten virgins, will be, as I have said, *preachers.* They are the third group; they are not asleep. The ten virgins—wise and foolish—were asleep, even the wise virgins! A state of being *asleep* is the best description of the modern Church I can think of. Dr. Martyn Lloyd-Jones's description was apt too: "its superficiality." It comes to much the same thing. Superficial. Shallow. Asleep.

What I am stressing in this final chapter of my book is that there will be those who *can* prepare; they are *not* asleep. The one hundred and twenty referred to likely needed the ten days to get ready (see Acts 1:15). What we know for sure is that by the time the Day of Pentecost arrived, *"they were all together in one place"* (Acts 2:1). The implication could be that they were not all together in one place on the day Jesus ascended to Heaven. In other words, two things apparently developed over the next ten days: (1) they all got together in spirit, and (2) they all managed to be in the same place. It also could mean that they all had not been together in fellowship or in opinion.

THE IMPORTANCE OF UNITY

For example, Peter stood up to express his view that a successor to Judas Iscariot needed to be found. I will not enter deeply into the discussion whether Peter was in the flesh or Spirit in his opinion. One of my predecessors at Westminster Chapel, G. Campbell Morgan, took the view that Peter and the one hundred and twenty were hasty; they unnecessarily voted for Matthias since Matthias was never mentioned again in the book of Acts (see Acts 1:21-26). That is a valid opinion, but we won't know until we get to Heaven whether the vote for Matthias was God's idea. But this *does* lead us to wonder if there was some division among the one hundred and twenty that they needed to get "all together."

That said, *"they were all together in one place"* on the Day of Pentecost. Whatever is implied in Luke's description of the one hundred and twenty, it certainly indicates unity. I cannot but think of these words of David:

> *Behold, how good and pleasant it is when brothers dwell in unity! It is like the precious oil on the head, running down on the beard, on the beard of Aaron, running down on the collar of his robes! It is like the dew of Hermon, which falls on the mountains of Zion! For there the Lord has commanded the blessing, life forevermore* (Psalm 133:1-3).

The words *"For there the Lord has commanded the blessing"* tell me that unity is a prerequisite for the blessing of God—indeed, the blessing of Pentecost. I have also thought how messy and sticky it would be to have oil on a beard! But sometimes unity is often preceded by going outside one's comfort zone.

FIVE THINGS WE CAN DO AS WE PREPARE FOR ISAAC

What, then, can those do who are awake and anticipate the midnight cry? I think of the words of Donald Gray Barnhouse (1895–1960): "While we wait, we can worship." I suggest five things you the reader might do:

1. *Show lavishness in thanksgiving and praise.*

Luke says that after Jesus' ascension, His followers *"worshiped him and returned to Jerusalem with great joy, and were continually in the temple blessing God"* (Luke 24:52-53). Taking the time to show thanks can be a sacrifice (see Ps. 50:23; Heb. 13:15). Paul urged us to put our requests to God *"with thanksgiving"* (Phil. 4:6). I would urge: Take time to thank God. Take time to reflect every day on how good God has been to you and how many things He does all the time. By the way, a few years ago the Mayo Clinic came up with an amazing conclusion: Thankful people live longer!

2. *Avoid bitterness at all costs.*

When Paul admonished us not to grieve the Spirit of God, the first thing he mentioned after that was to avoid *"bitterness"* (Eph. 4:30-31).

Bitterness is inward anger; it is holding a grudge. This sort of thing grieves the Holy Spirit. The Greek word translated *grieve* (*lupeite*) means "getting your feelings hurt." The Holy Spirit is a very, very sensitive person. I stress this in my book *Sensitivity of the Spirit* (Charisma House). Grieving the Holy Spirit is the easiest thing in the world to do! My advice: Find out what grieves the Spirit and don't do that! You have your work cut out for you. But it is worth the effort. The writer to the Hebrews warns against a *"root of bitterness"* springing up in us (Heb. 12:15).

3. *Learn to detect a rival spirit in yourself.*

The ungrieved Spirit in me will discern an ungrieved Spirit in you. The Holy Spirit will bring ultimate and total glory to God. The God of glory is unashamedly a jealous God (see Exod. 34:14; Acts 7:1). This will enable you to be detached from the will to receive personal praise. The sin that caused Israel to miss their Messiah—receiving glory from one another rather than seeking the praise of *"the only God"*—will cause you to forfeit usefulness in the next great move of God (John 5:44). Part of the preparation for the coming of Isaac is recognizing and eschewing the desire for the praise of people. The jealousy of God is a no-joke matter; He will not give His glory to another (see Isa. 42:8). It is a sobering thought that God will not bend the rules for any of us.

4. Practice total forgiveness non-stop, twenty-four hours a day, seven days a week.

The hardest thing in the world to do is to let your enemy completely off the hook. This means overlooking a fault or offense in another. Indeed, it is your glory: It is your *"glory to overlook an offense"* (Prov. 19:11). When your best friend—or mentor—betrays you; when your spouse was unfaithful to you; when you were raped, maligned, or laughed at; when you were threatened or lied about, you forgive them totally. Suggestion: Impute blood to their offense and show true godliness: *"When I see the blood, I will pass over you"* (Exod. 12:13). Pass over—overlook—their offense by praying the blessing of God on them. What is more, that is your glory!

5. Finally, let your conversation—your speech with anyone, your words to any human being—"always be gracious, seasoned with salt, so that you may know how you ought to answer each person" (Col. 4:6).

As you utter the message contained in the midnight cry, you will need to be both gracious and firm. *"Seasoned with salt"* means demonstrating both truth and grace, speaking in a spirit of meekness (Gal. 6:1). You will be required to give an answer to many (see 1 Pet. 3:15). Indeed, you will speak as one speaks the *"oracles of God"* (1 Pet. 4:11). You might say, "Me? Could a nobody like me speak the oracles of God?" Yes. This is because the same ungrieved Spirit that was renewed in the once cowardly Simon Peter and caused Jews to be afraid is alive and well today.

God will take ordinary, untrained, educated, and uneducated people to cause the rich, the poor, the famous, the wicked, the movie star, the politician to stand in awe of you. Apart from speaking with power, you will command demons to leave, the lame to walk, and dead people to arise. This will bring about more fear of God than ever. Millions will turn to God.

Then follows the second coming when every eye shall see Him; people will weep and wail and gnash their teeth. There follows the final judgment (see Heb. 9:27). Transparent and impartial justice will be carried out for the first time in history. God will clear His name. There will be no more crying, no more pain, and no more death.

As John said, *"These words are trustworthy and true"* (Rev. 21:5). This is because the integrity of God is at stake.

Conclusion

May the grace of our Lord Jesus Christ, the love of the God of glory, and the fellowship and the sprinkling of the blood of Jesus by the Holy Spirit be with you all evermore. Amen.

EPILOGUE

I closed the introduction of this book with the words "I am not a prophet. I am a Bible teacher."

Given you have now finished the book, I hope it was clear to you that I wrote this from a teacher's perspective through a biblical lens. I have tried to show *scripturally* why I have such conviction that the greatest move of the Spirit is yet to come.

However, it may surprise you to know that my convictions in this book don't rest solely on Scripture. My convictions have also been reinforced through a number of visions that I have had throughout my life.

When I was twenty years old, I was surprised to have an experience with the Holy Spirit that would change my life—including my theology—forever. As I drove down route 41, the glory of the Lord suddenly filled my car. Jesus was in the car with me interceding for me (see Heb. 13:15)! He was more real than anything around me. Over an hour later, around 7.45 a.m., I heard Jesus say to the Father, "He wants it." The Father replied, "He can have it."

I much later came to grasp what "it" was; I had entered into the rest of faith described in Hebrews 4:10—a peace and joy that I did not know were possible. I saw the face of Jesus looking at me for about a minute. By sundown the same day, I was conscious of two major theological changes: (1) I knew without doubt I was eternally saved; I could never be lost; and (2) I entered into an embryonic understanding of the sovereignty of God and predestination.

These were totally new concepts for me. I wondered if I had discovered something new! That perhaps I was the first since the apostle Paul to believe these things! I had not yet read a single book by any Calvinist. I found myself reading the Bible with an unthreatened openness to whatever it said as opposed to looking for support for what I wanted to believe. It led me to believe in the infallibility of the Bible. As I write this, it's curious to note that the one thing I am known most for (my Reformed theology) came in a vision! This is something that is not often associated with Reformed theologians! God truly has a sense of humor!

The presence of God during that visitation was real—very real—for some ten months. During this time, I had a series of nine or ten visions. Permit me to share a few of them briefly for context, and then I will share two others pertinent to the thesis of this book.

I had a vision of me preaching in New York City. Another vision was of my father coming to hear me preach, but I had no idea where; he was wearing a mint-green suit; it was a small church with a center aisle and with windows on one side only. Peculiarly, I had two visions of car dashboards—one was of an old Hudson, the other of an old Chevrolet. At the time, these meant nothing to me.

However, as I have journeyed through life, all these visions have been fulfilled! Within two months, I had resigned from my job as a pastor and needed a way to pay my bills. A man named Marvin Creamens overheard that I needed a job. He offered me a job driving his truck for Creamens Quality Cleaners. As soon as I got in the truck, there was the vision fulfilled that had made no sense: the exact Chevrolet dashboard as in the vision. Around the same time, I needed a car and was given an old Hudson I could make use of. As soon as I slid into the driver's seat of the car—you guessed it—I saw the exact same dashboard I had seen only weeks earlier! Both of these experiences gave me great relief to see afresh that I was in the will of God, all thanks to a vision.

Some four or five years after these visions, I became the pastor of the Fairview Church of God in Carlisle, Ohio. The church had a center aisle and windows on one side only. On my second Sunday, my dad came to hear me preach. Before he arrived, I said to Louise, "My father will be wearing a mint-green suit. He will walk down the center aisle of the church at some point during the time he is there." When he came to our house in Carlisle, he handed me his mint-green suit on a hanger. The next day after the morning service, there he came walking down the center aisle.

Several years ago, I developed a special relationship with Tim Dilena, who is the pastor of Times Square Church in New York City. Since July 2021, I have been preaching monthly at his church—another fulfillment of those visions.

Again, I am not a prophet. I am a Bible teacher. Some of these visions were fulfilled in mere months, some took a few years, yet others took more than sixty years to be fulfilled. But there are two visions that have yet to come to pass; however, I believe with all my heart that they will, and I pray with all my heart I will be around to see their fulfillment.

In both these visions, I saw that great revival would go around the world with the message *Jesus is coming soon* and that people were shaken and believed it. The conviction that Isaac is coming was birthed from those visions, and this book is my best attempt to describe why it hasn't arrived yet and what it may look like when it does. Of course, I am not the only person to have seen visions like this, but I pray, dear reader, as you have read this book, that God has stirred your heart to not only see but be a part of this glorious end-time revival.

ABOUT R. T. KENDALL

- Born – July 13, 1935 in Ashland, Kentucky
- Married – to Louise Wallis of Sterling, Illinois on June 28, 1958
- Children – son Robert Tillman II (TR), married to Annette, daughter Melissa Tabb married to Rex Tabb.
- Three grandsons, Tobias, Timothy and Tyndale (Ty) Kendall
- A.B. Trevecca Nazarene University of Nashville, Tennessee 1970
- M.Div. Southern Baptist Theological Seminary, Louisville, Kentucky 1972
- M.A. University of Louisville, Louisville, Kentucky 1973
- D..Phil. Oxford University 1977
- D.D., Trevecca Nazarene University, 2008
- Senior Minister, Westminster Chapel, February 1, 1977 to February 1, 2002
- Author of many books.

Our premise is this. It seems to us that there has been a "silent divorce" in the church, speaking generally, between the Word and the Spirit. When there is a divorce, some children stay with the mother, some stay with the father.

In this divorce, there are those on the "word" side and those on the "Spirit" side. What is the difference?

Take those of us who represent the Word. Our message is this: we must earnestly contend for the faith "once delivered unto the saints" (Jude 3), we need get back to expository preaching, sound doctrine such as justification by faith, the sovereignty of God and the internal testimony of the Spirit as taught by men like Martin Luther, John Calvin and Jonathan Edwards. What is wrong with this emphasis? Nothing. It is exactly right.

Take those whose emphasis has been on the Holy Spirit. What is the message? We need to rediscover the power that was manifested in the Book of Acts, there needs to be a demonstration of signs, wonders and miracles; we need to see the gifts of the Spirit operating in the church – that the world will once again take notice of the church so that people are left without excuse. What is wrong with this emphasis? Nothing. It is exactly right.

We believe that the need of the hour is not one or the other – but both! It is our view that this simultaneous combination will result in spontaneous combustion! And then, but almost certainly only then, will the world be shaken once again by the message of the church.

This was the message I have preached over the years at Westminster Chapel in London. This is what we are endeavoring to preach in America and around the world. This is not all we preach but it is certainly one of the main things we preach alongside the need for total forgiveness and learning to be sensitive to the voice of the Holy Spirit. We need your prayers. God bless you.

—Dr. R.T. Kendall

From

R.T. Kendall

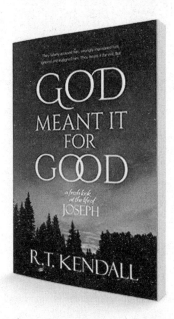

British pastor R.T. Kendall analyzes the Old Testament story of Joseph to bring comfort and hope to those who have been misused, falsely accused, humiliated, abandoned, or otherwise afflicted by showing how God can turn evil to good.

Purchase your copy wherever books are sold

From
John & Carol Arnott

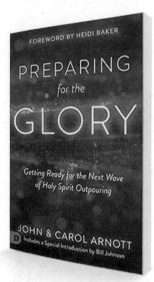

A fresh move of God is on the horizon!

In the midst of fear, conflict, and unrest, a great Kingdom light is piercing through the darkness. Since the Day of Pentecost, this light of Holy Spirit outpouring has been increasing in brightness and will soon break forth in an unprecedented outpouring of supernatural glory.

Are you prepared for what God wants to release in these last days?

Preparing for the Glory is a groundbreaking new work from John and Carol Arnott that shares practical keys, gleaned from over 20 years of leading a global revival movement, that will position you to expect and experience this new move of God!

Learn how to:

- Stay hungry for God by maintaining a passionate desire to encounter His presence, no matter how spiritually dry or distant you feel.
- Press in for deeper experiences with the Spirit by "feeding" yourself on supernatural testimonies of God's work.
- Embrace the fear of the Lord--the key that will unlock an increase of glory manifestations, unusual miracles, and Holy Spirit fire.

Prepare your life to be a resting place for the Holy Spirit in this historic hour of glory, presence, and miracles!

Purchase your copy wherever books are sold

Check out
our **Destiny Image**
bestsellers page at
destinyimage.com/bestsellers

for cutting-edge,
prophetic messages
that will supernaturally
empower you and the
body of Christ.

YOUR Prophetic COMMUNITY

Sign up for **FREE** Subscription to the Destiny Image
digital magazine, and get awesome content
delivered directly to your inbox!
destinyimage.com/signup

Sign-up for Cutting-Edge Messages that Supernaturally Empower You

• Gain valuable insights and guidance based on biblical principles
• Deepen your faith and understanding of God's plan for your life
• Receive regular updates and prophetic messages
• Connect with a community of believers who share your values and beliefs

Experience Fresh Video Content that Strengthens Your Prophetic Inheritance

• Receive prophetic messages and insights
• Connect with a powerful tool for spiritual growth and development
• Stay connected and inspired on your faith journey

Listen to Powerful Podcasts that Equips You for God's Presence Everyday

• Deepen your understanding of God's prophetic assignment
• Experience God's revival power throughout your day
• Learn how to grow spiritually in your walk with God

In the Right Hands, This Book Will Change Lives!

Most of the people who need this message will not be looking for this book. To change their lives, you need to **put a copy of this book in their hands.**

Our ministry is constantly seeking methods to find the people who need this anointed message to change their lives. **Will you help us reach these people?**

Extend this ministry by sowing 3 books, 5 books, 10 books, or more today, and become a life changer! Your generosity will be part of catalyzing the Great Awakening that many have been prophesying and praying for.